Presented To

Mildred Amadeo

On

May 9, 2010

By

Noemi, Liana, Samaria and Daniel

LIFE ON PURPOSE™ DEVOTIONAL FOR MOTHERS

Practical Faith and Profound Insight for Every Day

By

Harrison House

Harrison House
Tulsa, OK

09 08 07 06 05   10 9 8 7 6 5 4 3 2 1

Life on Purpose Devotional for Mothers:
Practical Faith and Profound Insight for Every Day
ISBN 1-57794-683-9
Copyright © 2005 by Harrison House, Inc.

Published by Harrison House, Inc.
P.O. Box 35035
Tulsa, OK 74153

Contents

Introduction

Before we were born, God reserved a specific purpose for each of us. As mothers, we know a little something about purpose. We realize, for example, that it was not mere chance that made us mothers. We understand that specific events, supernatural intervention, and more than a little human effort brought children into our lives. It was by God's design that we accepted the privilege and responsibility of motherhood, and it is only with His continuing presence that we will fulfill His purpose in this role.

God's purpose for each of us is unique and wonderful, and when we discover it we begin to understand how much all of creation means to Him. We glimpse the potential of each moment He has given us and, simultaneously, the absolute necessity of leaning on His strength to further His plan.

In that gracious plan, God has accounted for the hectic, the dull, the momentous, and the ordinary moments of our day-to-day lives. He sees our schedules and He sees our limitations, yet each day He invites us to know Him and to make Him known. Our availability is all He requires.

Today, God invites us to continue a journey toward deeper intimacy with Him and a greater understanding of His plan for us, for our children, and for all of creation. He welcomes us to set aside our inhibitions and to internalize His ability to accomplish His will. Through these pages, He bids us to discover *Life on Purpose for Mothers.*

In God's House

One thing I ask of the Lord, this is what I seek: that I may dwell in the house of the Lord all the days of my life, to gaze upon the beauty of the Lord and to seek him in his temple.

PSALM 27:4

Your alarm clock has just sounded, and you roll over to turn it off. Your mind starts working, remembering the state you left the home in before bed after an especially long day yesterday. The dirty laundry pile is cascading over the top of the hamper, the children's papers and sneakers are strewn across the entrance, dishes are settled on one side of the kitchen sink, and the plumber is scheduled to arrive in an hour to fix the garbage disposal. You're tempted to roll over in bed and just forget it all, tranquilizing your mind with sleep.

But as you reach to reset your alarm for five more minutes of precious slumber, your arm brushes a Book you've set there for moments just like these. Its wisdom and peace beckon you, resounding past the mental commotion and reaching deeper within to your spirit, which recognizes the priceless opportunity before you: a moment in God's presence. Suddenly, thoughts of your earthly home and concerns vanish as you open the Book and find Him there.

David knew the agony of waking up to disarray and mental commotion, but he wrote, "One thing I ask of the Lord, this is what I seek: that I may dwell in the house of the Lord all the days of my life, to gaze upon the beauty of the Lord and to seek him in his temple" (Ps. 27:4). While running for his very life from King Saul, whose kingship God had reassigned to him, David spent many nights in caves and under the open desert sky. Laundry, sneakers, and dishes would have been a welcome sight to a fugitive whose daily and nightly concerns were rattlesnakes, swords, and a madman!

The one thing that kept David going was the thought of home—not the cave and not the palace, but the very presence of the Lord. Above everything in this world, David longed for time in God's house.

Do you long for time in God's house? Sometimes life can numb our minds to the longing of our spirits. The reason David's spirit pulled him so strongly toward God's house was that he knew from repeated experience the amazing benefits available there. He knew God's house offered light, salvation, beauty, safety, exaltation, mercy, instruction, goodness—and more. (See Ps. 27.)

Do you know what God's house contains for you? Like David, you can become personally aware of the benefits of time in God's presence. You can choose to dwell in God's house—every day. For just a few minutes, you can let your spirit indulge in what you need most: a moment in God's presence. It's not that you'll neglect your earthly responsibilities.

LIVE ON PURPOSE TODAY

Spend time in God's house today, and He will help you manage yours.

Contrarily, as you live in God's house on a continual basis, you'll find everything you need to perform the responsibilities God has called you to do each day.

So before you roll over for five more minutes of sleep to forget about the mess and before you dash out of bed to tackle all of it, why don't you satisfy the longing of your spirit and find the strength in God to do whatever you have to do today? Grab the Book and get on your knees for some time in God's house. You'll be glad you did.

PRAYER

*Lord, help me to recognize the longing in my heart for
Your presence. I know that in Your presence is fullness of joy,
and that You offer me life more abundantly. When I'm
overwhelmed, remind me that You're here for me always and
I can dwell above distress when I dwell in Your house eternally.
In Jesus' name, I dedicate this time to You. Amen.*

You Can Do This!

*But now, this is what the Lord says—he who created you,
O Jacob, he who formed you, O Israel: "Fear not, for I have
redeemed you; I have summoned you by name; you are mine."*

ISAIAH 43:1

The Bible tells us many times, "Fear not," but motherhood often challenges our will to remain fearless. Do you remember when your toddler tried to run toward a busy street, when your grade-schooler went to summer camp for the first time, or when your teenager grabbed the keys and set out on his first solo car drive? Each time, something inside of you wanted to pull your child back into the shelter of your arms forever, safe from all harm.

And, all this time, weighing more heavily on you than the desire to keep your kids safe from physical harm has been the desire to protect them from emotional and spiritual harm. You were privileged to see them enter this world with pure minds and unbroken hearts, and you want that wholeness to remain. Yet the world they live in lures them toward impurity and slings arrows of pain and brokenness toward their hearts.

Then comes the question in your own heart: "Can I really do this? Can I be the mother God wants me to be for these children?"

In Isaiah 43:1, God speaks to His chosen people, "Fear not, for I have redeemed you; I have summoned you by name; you are mine." You are not only one of God's chosen, but you are His choice to be the mother of the children He has entrusted to your care. In the great, eternal plan of God, it is no accident that you are the mother of your children. God summoned you by name to mother them, and He says, "Fear not.... You are mine."

God did not lightly give you the calling to mother your children, and He has not left you empty-handed for the task. The equipment is within you and before you. Not only did He give you the natural instincts to nurture your children as they grow physically, but as a daughter of God you have His supernatural ability within you to rise above the limitations of this world and guide your children into wholeness of spirit, soul, and body. You also have access to the wisdom of His Word—the Bible—to guide you each step of the way.

When your kids begin to move beyond the safety of your reach, or when you doubt your ability to nurture them as God wants you to, run to the One who has said, "Fear not! I called you, I have equipped you, and you are Mine." In His arms, you will find both the comfort and the strength you need to finish the task He has given you. In His presence, you will discover a victorious God who protects His children— even when you cannot.

LIVE ON PURPOSE TODAY

In the Word, find your God-given equipment for the task of mothering your children. For example, see James 1:5; Proverbs 24:3-4; Galatians 5:22-23; and Ephesians 6:10-18.

PRAYER

Lord, You know better than I the plans You have for each of my children, so teach me how to nurture them. In the difficult moments, thank You for holding me close and reassuring me that You have called and equipped me for the task. I will seek You daily for the strength and wisdom I need, in Jesus' name. Amen.

Raising Up God's Champions

Then I heard the voice of the Lord saying, "Whom shall I send? And who will go for us?" And I said, "Here am I. Send me!"

ISAIAH 6:8

From Noah to Abraham to David and beyond, God has always been a champion builder—and when He looks at your kids, He sees the same champion Spirit within them that led each of these great people of faith into victories for Him.

Several characteristics set God's champions apart.

First, God's champions know His voice. When we train our children to hear God's voice, we give them a vital key to becoming His champions. Because God's spoken word in the heart will always be confirmed in His written Word, our first step in raising up God's champions is to give them His Word.

Second, God's champions believe His promise and follow His leading no matter what. Consider the odds against the faith of God's great Old Testament champions. Though no rain had ever fallen on earth in the history of humankind, Noah believed God would send a flood and, therefore, built the ark. Though he was childless at one hundred years old, Abraham believed God would make him a father of many nations. Though seemingly nothing but a scrawny teenager, David believed God would use him to slay a giant and concisely win a war for God's people. Because of the unwavering faith of each of these men, God won irrevocable victories through each one.

Third, God's champions expect to win. First Corinthians 9:24 says, "Do you not know that in a race all the runners run, but only one gets the prize? Run in such a way as to get the prize." When your children learn—from the Word and from personal experience—that God is a winner, and all who follow Him are winners, His victory is the only thing they expect.

Fourth, God's champions understand that His anointing enables them to win. Psalm 23:5 in *The Amplified Bible* says, "You anoint my head with oil; my [brimming] cup runs over." The footnote on this verse discloses the power of this imagery:

LIVE ON PURPOSE TODAY

Today, tell your kids about one of God's champions from His Word. Then tell them that they, too, are His champions.

...it was customary in hot climates to anoint the body with oil to protect it from excessive perspiration. When mixed with perfume, the oil imparted a delightfully refreshing and invigorating sensation. Athletes anointed their bodies as a matter of course before running a race. As the body, therefore, anointed with oil was refreshed, invigorated, and better fitted for action, so the Lord would anoint His 'sheep' with the Holy Spirit, Whom oil symbolizes, to fit them to engage more freely in His service and run in the way He directs—in heavenly fellowship with Him.

When our children are anointed with the Holy Spirit for the tasks God gives them, they are empowered to win every time.

Finally, God's champions give Him all the glory. The apostle John reveals to us what happens when we give God the glory for the victories He enables us to win:

> Whenever the living creatures give glory, honor and thanks to him who sits on the throne and who lives for ever and ever, the twenty-four elders fall down before him who sits on the throne, and worship him who lives for ever and ever. They lay their crowns before the throne and say: "You are worthy, our Lord and God, to receive glory and honor and power, for you created all things, and by your will they were created and have their being."
>
> REVELATION 4:9-11

Each of your children is marked as a champion who brings glory, honor, and power to God's name. God calls out today, "Whom shall I send? And who will go for us?" Raise up your children to hear His voice, so that they can respond in unwavering faith, "Here am I. Send me!" (Isa. 6:8). Then get ready to see victory after victory won for God's kingdom through each one of your kids—His champions.

PRAYER

Father, in Jesus' name, here am I; send me to raise up this new generation of champions for You. I dedicate to teaching my kids Your Word so they can know, believe, and act on Your will— bringing glory, honor, and power to Your name. Amen.

In His Hands

See, I have inscribed you on the palms of My hands;
Your walls are continually before Me.

ISAIAH 49:16

Many people define themselves by what they do: "I'm a doctor," "I'm a receptionist," "I'm a mom," and so forth. For whatever reason, we often place varying degrees of importance on each title and fight for a position (at least in our own minds) at "the top." This doesn't apply just to entrepreneurs and CEOs; we mothers can be among the fiercest competitors for a position at the top.

The truth is that we all want validation for what we do, and often motherhood can be a thankless job. While we're picking up the stray pieces of corn all over the floor after our toddler's dinner, he isn't kneeling beside us saying, "Thanks, Mom!" More likely, he's pouring puzzle pieces all over his room! Or when we hear the engine turn off in the driveway and open the door to our teenager at midnight after sitting up worried, she doesn't say, "Thanks, Mom!" She's probably walking briskly to her room, hoping to avoid our questions.

Yes, motherhood is often a thankless job—if we're looking for verbal thanks. And, yes, we can and should train our kids to say "thank you." But as wonderful as their verbal gratitude may be, it can only give us a temporary boost to continue with the enormous task of motherhood. What we really need is something we cannot receive from anyone on earth. It is something only available from heaven.

The Bible says that we are not to work for the applause of human beings, but for God alone. Jesus said, "Be careful not to do your 'acts of righteousness' before men, to be seen by them. If you do, you will have no reward from your Father in heaven" (Matt. 6:1). The reward from our Father in heaven is of much more value than the temporary reward of human recognition.

Our heavenly reward is, in part, the deep satisfaction of knowing that God is pleased with us not just for what we do but for who we are. And we are not the titles we may give ourselves—doctor, receptionist, mom, and so forth—we are something more. We are His.

When we realize this, we will find the peace that God has provided for us. We will understand that we are not defined by what we do as mothers, or as businesswomen, or as anything else, but by our relationship with God. We will remain steady not only when our children's needs press us beyond our human limitations, but also when they are no longer our daily demand—when our children have left home and our job description under the "mother" title has completely changed. We

LIVE ON PURPOSE TODAY

Locate some Scriptures that define you as God sees you. For example, see Deuteronomy 28:1-14; Isaiah 43:1; 2 Corinthians 2:14; and Ephesians 5:1.

will no longer strive for a place at the elusive top. We will realize that, like all of God's children, we are already right where we need to be—in His hands.

PRAYER

Lord, thank You for the reward that You alone can give me for the duties I perform as Your servant on this earth. Holy Spirit, thank You for encouraging me in this season of my life, showing me who I am in You. I will do everything as unto You, and not for human recognition. I will acknowledge, honor, and glorify You in everything I say and do, in Jesus' name. Amen.

Are You Playing the Harp or Just Plain Harping?

BY KATHY PRIDE

> *I praise you with the harp for your faithfulness, O my God;*
> *I will sing praise to you with the lyre, O Holy One of Israel.*
>
> PSALM 71:22

What kinds of sounds come out of your lips? Are you clanging like an out-of-tune gong, or are you making beautiful music? I am learning to turn the discordant sounds of a screeching violin into the soft and gentle melodies of a harp.

I had nagging down to an art form, a finer art form, at that. And we know what the Bible says about nagging: "…a quarrelsome wife is like a constant dripping" (Prov. 19:13). For years I lived with the misguided notion that if I harassed, nagged, whined, or screamed long enough and loud enough, whatever behavior or decision I disagreed with would change. My voice was shrill and harsh, demanding and insistent. Oh, and did I mention repetitive? It wasn't enough to simply remind or direct, it was incessant reminders and direction. The question became how many annoying ways could I possibly come up with to say the same thing. When I was ignored, which was usually the case, I frequently added a dose of sarcasm to my words in an attempt to prompt a response. I could even embellish with facial expressions and hand gestures. It was harping in its purest form.

Slowly I have learned, and am continuing to learn, to play the harp. I try to keep my voice even and on the quiet side, devoid of any edginess. I try to listen and not interrupt and harass those who are speaking. Even when I am angry I attempt to speak the truth in love. That means not using sarcasm, and not reverting to harsh tones and accusations. Rather, I attempt to monitor and choose my words carefully, and offer constructive suggestions when asked. I would much rather uplift than harass, yet when I revert to harping it is generally out of fear or insecurity. I hate losing the illusion of maintaining control. Notice I use the word "try." I am far from perfect and fail often.

When I start to harp and nag I need to think about what those insecurities and fears are: Am I unsure of my parenting posture? Am I unsure of my convictions? Am I succumbing to manipulation by my child? Am I afraid of being snubbed or rebuffed?

LIVE ON PURPOSE TODAY

Begin each day in prayer, asking God specifically to remind you when you are harping instead of playing the harp, and that your ear can recognize the difference.

It is much more difficult to play the harp than just plain harp, but it is so much more fruitful to find the more harmonious way. When I guard my tongue and speak gently, I am much more apt to generate an honest response from those with whom I am in communication. The open communication I yearn for is a two-way street—one I need to remember to travel.

PRAYER

God, help me to avoid the discordant sounds of nagging and harassing as a way of prompting action. Help me to walk in love and manifest the fruit of Your Spirit on a daily basis. Let me be quick to listen and slow to speak. Help me use my voice to generate sounds pleasing to Your ears. In Jesus' name I pray. Amen.

What's Inside?

Tell those who are rich in this world not to be proud and not to trust in their money, which will soon be gone. But their trust should be in the living God, who richly gives us all we need for our enjoyment.

1 TIMOTHY 6:17 NLT

Maybe we've all done it: watched a commercial, seen an advertisement, or walked through the mall, and started getting caught up in our outward appearance. We think, *My jeans don't fit right... I need a manicure...a pedicure...a facial... I could really use some new shoes... I need to work out! I look like I've had a kid, or two, or three....* If we don't stop ourselves with this focus on our outward appearance, we can get lost in other outward concerns as well—our cars, our houses, and our family's possessions. If it doesn't stop there, we can start to obsess about our savings accounts and retirement funds!

God certainly desires to bless His children with the materials necessary to enjoy life. (See 1 Tim. 6:17.) However, He never intended for those things to be our focus. Far from it, for Jesus specifically said,

> "Do not worry, saying, 'What shall we eat?' or 'What shall we drink?' or 'What shall we wear?' For after all these things the Gentiles seek. For your heavenly Father knows that you need all these things. Seek first the kingdom of

God and His righteousness, and all these things shall be added to you."

MATTHEW 6:31-33 NKJV

Furthermore, when it came to material possessions, the apostles of the New Testament church focused most on giving them away. For example, 1 John 3:17 says, "If anyone has material possessions and sees his brother in need but has no pity on him, how can the love of God be in him?" (See also Rom. 15:27 and 1 Cor. 9:11.)

Many people have worked so hard for every penny in their possession that they start to cling to their material wealth like a trophy. Even when people have leaned on God to help them through the penniless days to come to the days of plenty, they sometimes forget God in the end. God warned the people of Israel of this very thing:

> You may say to yourself, "My power and the strength of my hands have produced this wealth for me." But remember the Lord your God, for it is he who gives you the ability to produce wealth....

DEUTERONOMY 8:17,18

Today, remember that God is the One who gives you the power to gain wealth, and pray that He would show you what He wants you to do with it. It's wonderful to look beautiful, to have nice things, and to be able to provide for our families. In fact, God wants those things for us. However, we must always keep our focus on what's inside.

What matters is not your outer appearance—the styling of your hair, the jewelry you wear, the cut of your clothes—but your inner disposition. Cultivate inner beauty, the gentle, gracious kind that God delights in.

1 PETER 3:3,4 MESSAGE

What is inside of you? More specifically, who is inside? If Jesus is inside, He has become your righteousness. (1 Cor. 1:30.)

When you set your focus on Jesus, you set your focus on the kingdom of God and His righteousness, and this is when "all these things shall be added to you" (Matt. 6:33 NKJV).

LIVE ON PURPOSE TODAY

Decide today to stop thinking about yourself and focus on how you can bless others.

Next time your outward needs and desires holler for your attention, allow your spirit to refocus your attention on what really matters: what's inside. Allow the inner beauty of Christ to touch everything in your life so that His kingdom comes and His will is done on earth, in your life, as it is in heaven.

PRAYER

Lord, thank You for being my provider. I seek You and Your righteousness first in my life, and I trust You to supply all my needs. Thank You, Holy Spirit, for imparting Your wisdom and ability to me and my husband so that we can acquire and distribute materials that bring enjoyment and provision to our family and those to whom You lead us to give, in Jesus' name. Amen.

The Gift We Give Back

Children are a gift from the Lord; they are a reward from him.

PSALM 127:3 NLT

Children are a gift from the Lord, and we are privileged as parents to present them back to Him. As we train our children in His ways, leading them into His presence, they become beautiful vessels for His use.

A mother's opportunity to encourage her child's spiritual connection to the Father begins at her child's conception. A baby in the womb can hear and respond to external noises from the outside world and move to the rhythm of his mother's speech.[1] If his physical body can receive (through hearing) and respond (with motion) to the sounds around him, how much more can his spirit receive and respond to the surrounding spiritual environment?

The Bible promises us that when we gather together in Jesus' name, He is in our midst. (Matt. 18:20.) Jesus' presence heals, restores, saves, and matures every person who spends time with Him. From the womb to high school graduation and beyond, your child will benefit from time in God's presence.

Even before your child can speak, he can become acquainted with the Scriptures when he regularly hears you speak them. Toddlers can memorize Scripture, especially when it is reinforced with motions or music. In fact, a child will learn any new biblical concept best when it reaches several of his senses—hearing, touch, sight, smell, and taste. That's why teaching tools like music, rhythm and rhyme, body movement, pictures, and object lessons, such as communion, are so effective.

God, the Master Teacher, has always used various methods to impress His Word on the hearts of His people. For example, He told His children, "Fix these words of mine in your hearts and minds; tie them as symbols on your hands and bind them on your foreheads" (Deut. 11:18). These symbols on the Israelites' hands and foreheads reached their senses of sight and touch and instilled within them the words of God. Even today, we can "bind" a symbol of God's Word to our kids with a sticker, a T-shirt, or a piece of jewelry that they carry on their person all day, reminding them of the biblical truths they have learned.

Again addressing the sense of sight, God continued instructing the children of Israel, "Write [my words] on the doorframes of your houses and on your gates" (v. 20). The Israelites literally painted His words on their walls and gates, and His words became emblazoned on the memory of every member of each

LIVE ON PURPOSE TODAY

If your family doesn't presently share a consistent daily devotional time, initiate one today.

family. Through the creative use of visual aids in our homes, we too can deeply instill God's Word in our children.

As we teach our children, using our words, worshipful music, object lessons, and other teaching tools, we will be blessed to watch their personal relationship with Him grow. Colossians 1:28 summarizes our ultimate goal:

> We warn them and teach them with all the wisdom
> God has given us, for we want to present them to God,
> perfect [or *mature*] in their relationship to Christ.

As we lovingly feed our children God's Word, their sense of identity and purpose grows. They become mature in their relationship with Christ. Then we are privileged to give back to Him the precious gifts He gave us——each one complete, whole, and perfect in Him.

PRAYER

Father, thank You for the gift of each one of my children. Use me, Lord, to lead them into Your presence every day. I commit to feed them Your Word, their daily bread. Help me to make the most of every opportunity to teach them Your ways. Thank You for bringing the Word back to their remembrance each time they need it and for perfecting and maturing them, in Jesus' name. Amen.

A Sure Foundation

BY ANN PLATZ

*And no one can ever lay any other real foundation
than that one we already have—Jesus Christ.*

1 CORINTHIANS 3:11 TLB

A master builder will quickly point out the importance of the right foundation for any building project. A poor footing will not support a building. Structural problems will have to be remedied, usually at great expense. In most cases, it is better to tear down such a house and rebuild it.

When my husband, John, and I were house-hunting once, I took him to see a charming cottage with a guest house that I thought would be perfect for our needs. He checked it out and later told me that he suspected weaknesses in the structure and that whoever bought it would have problems. My husband was so right! A year later, when I drove by that property, I learned that the new owners had torn the house down and were building a new one on the site.

Laying the right spiritual foundation is most critical. Even as a child I was aware of my need for a Savior, and through the years I have learned to rely on His faithfulness.

A woman who builds her life on Jesus Christ knows that He is the chief Cornerstone. To build on anything but the Rock

LIVE ON PURPOSE TODAY

Is every part of your life built upon the foundation of Jesus Christ? If not, commit every part to Him today.

is to build a house on sand. "For when the rains and floods come, and storm winds beat against [her] house, it will fall with a mighty crash" (Matt. 7:27 TLB).

The wise woman knows where to build. "Though the rain comes in torrents, and the floods rise and the storm winds beat against [her] house, it won't collapse, for it is built on rock" (v. 25 TLB).[2]

PRAYER

Father, I have chosen to build my life and my family upon the Rock, the chief Cornerstone, Jesus Christ. Jesus, because You are our sure foundation, we remain strong no matter what rises against us. Thank You, Lord, that through every season of life You hold us in place and give us Your perfect peace, in Jesus' name. Amen.

Let Him Love Through You

May he be enthroned in God's presence forever;
appoint your love and faithfulness to protect him.

PSALM 61:7

I n 1 Corinthians 12, Paul tells us that the body of Christ is composed of many members, each operating in a significant function. Some prophesy, for example, and some teach. At the end of the chapter, however, Paul concludes that one function is more significant than any of these. It is love. The best thing about love is that we can all operate in it. In fact, in order to be effective in our specific assignments, we must.

No matter what your gift and calling may be, you are called and equipped to love. For the role of motherhood, the significance of love is apparent. A mother's body is designed to nurture her child from the moment of his conception. At birth, her child continues to depend on her. Without her nurturing response to his physical needs, she risks losing him. Even then, while she can provide the food and shelter necessary for his physical survival, more is required for his emotional and spiritual survival. Every child needs love.

Beyond a child's need to receive love is the mother's need to be motivated by it. She can nurture her child only to a limited degree without the inner motivation of love. That is why, in all but rare cases, love comes so naturally to her.

As she continues to nurture her child with love, she begins to see love reflected back to her. The principle of sowing and reaping is constantly at work in her relationship with her child. If love is what we desire to reap from our children's lives, we need to make sure that love is what we sow into them.

Therefore, we need to know what love is—and what it is not. Love is not, for example, silently submitting to whatever our children do or whatever is done to them. Quite contrarily, it is taking an active position in their lives, guarding them with and imparting in them the nature of their heavenly Father.

Love is not passive but active. It is not weak but strong. The strength of love can be seen in 1 Corinthians 13:7 and Psalm 61:7, which both identify love as a protector. More than a protector, love is *everything* that God is—because God is love. This is what our children need, and this is what we can give them.

According to 2 Peter 1:3-4, "His divine power has given us everything we need for life and godliness through our knowledge of him who called us by his own glory and goodness. Through these he has given us his very great and precious promises, so that through them you may participate in the divine nature...." As participants in God's nature, we can love our children with God's love.

Yes, we will make mistakes. God knew we would, and He also knew that His grace would be sufficient for us. If we depend on Him, His love

LIVE ON PURPOSE TODAY

Allow God to love your children through your actions and words today.

will shine through our lives and be reflected back to us through our children's lives. We can depend on it, because His love never fails.

PRAYER

Father, in Jesus' name, I thank You for loving my children through me today. I have all the attributes of love inside because I am a participant in Your nature. I am patient and kind. I do not envy or boast. I am not proud, rude, self-seeking, or easily angered. I keep no record of wrongs. I do not delight in evil but rejoice with the truth. I always protect, always trust, always hope, always persevere. Your love working in and through me never fails. Amen.

Go for It

*Delight yourself in the Lord and he will give you
the desires of your heart.*

PSALM 37:4

So many times in life, we think, *Oh, if only I had time to do this,* or *If only I could have that.* And, though the thought comes to us repeatedly, we never do anything to fulfill that desire.

Let's say you've been thinking, *I need to spend some quiet time with God every day,* or *I would really like to start a business,* or *I wish I could play tennis.* Whatever your desire, if it's something you haven't yet accomplished, then you've probably considered a million reasons why you can't have what you want.

It happens to all of us, and as mothers our desires often come last on our priority lists. However, if we are to live the fulfilled and meaningful lives God desires for us, we can't just shrug off our desires. What we need to do is evaluate them to see whether they're worth our attention and effort to attain. Our first question should be, "Is this something God wants for me?"

Often, God is the One who plants desires in our hearts, sometimes for a purpose we cannot readily see. Psalm 37:4 says, "Delight yourself in the Lord and he will give you the desires of your heart." If you believe God has planted a desire in your heart, ask Him to help you fulfill that desire.

God plants desires in your heart, and He can fulfill them—when you press toward Him. Psalm 20:4 says, "May he give you the desire of your heart and make all your plans succeed." When you make plans to attain the desire He has given you, He will make your plans succeed.

God has good things in store for you. Today, commit to follow Him step by step into His ultimate plan. Start with one desire, and write it down. In Habakkuk 2:2, the Lord told the prophet, "Write the vision and make it plain on tablets, that he may run who reads it."

What vision has God given you? You are endowed with a unique purpose, and in order to fulfill that purpose you will need to press toward the desires God has given you. They may seem trivial, or they may seem unattainable, but don't neglect to reach for them as He leads you. One step in the right direction could catapult you into the next level of the calling on your life. Take a risk, and you'll realize it's no risk at all—because all of heaven backs you when you reach for God's desires.

LIVE ON PURPOSE TODAY

Write down your God-given vision, and take one step toward it today.

PRAYER

Father, I acknowledge the desires You've planted in my heart.
I pray that You would enlighten me by Your Word and
Your Spirit with wisdom to take steps toward their fulfillment.
Thank You, Lord, that You make my plans succeed because
I give You lordship in my life. I want only what You want for me.
Thank You for accomplishing great things in and through me
as I work with You, in Jesus' name. Amen.

Time With God in a Busy Schedule

*Impress them on your children. Talk about them
when you sit at home and when you walk along
the road, when you lie down and when you get up.*

DEUTERONOMY 6:7

With church, school, sports, clubs, lessons, and a flurry of other activities, our kids' lives can become very time-constrained. Nevertheless, we see the importance of their daily time in God's presence and we want to help them make room in their busy schedules for Him.

Thousands of years ago, God told His people to teach their children His commands. We may think times have changed, but His words seem custom fit for kids' busy schedules today:

> These commandments that I give you today are to be upon your hearts. Impress them on your children. Talk about them when you sit at home and when you walk along the road, when you lie down and when you get up.
>
> DEUTERONOMY 6:6,7

God wants us to impress His commands on our children, and we want to because we know the benefits available to those who follow Him. However, sometimes we don't see the opportunities to make that imprint on their hearts. Right here in Deuteronomy, God clearly identifies those opportunities: "Talk about them when you sit at home and when you walk along the road, when you lie down and when you get up" (v. 7). In other words, every time we're with our kids—in the living room, in the car, at the table, in the hallway, and so forth—we should be encouraging a dialogue with them about God's Word.

God requires us to help our kids begin and maintain a relationship with Him. Even when our schedules are busy, we can do that by establishing a relationship with our kids that always invites their questions and their insights about God. By our example and through our conversations, we can encourage our kids to remain in His presence all day, every day.

Psalm 91:1 and 9 speak of making God our shelter, our dwelling, and our refuge. We can teach our children to live their lives in Him through continual fellowship—interaction with Him—every day. One form of ongoing fellowship with God is praise. Psalm 34:1 NKJV says, "I will bless the Lord at all times; His praise shall continually be in my mouth." With music or with simple words of thanks to God, our kids can learn to live in a constant state of praising and acknowledging God.

Another form of perpetual interaction with God is prayer. First Thessalonians 5:17 says,

LIVE ON PURPOSE TODAY

Take every opportunity today to talk about God's Word with your kids.

"Pray without ceasing." When we make prayer an ongoing part of our lives, we can help our children see the necessity and the benefits of daily communion with Him.

Whether we have five minutes or five hours with our kids, we can bring God's Word into our conversation and help them build their relationship with Him. When we remain alert to the opportunities God so clearly pointed out to us so many years ago, we give our children the priceless gift of a vibrant relationship with Him—and we give Him another generation to carry His love to the next.

PRAYER

Father, in Jesus' name, I thank You for all the opportunities You've given me to teach my children Your Word. Holy Spirit, enlighten their minds as they hear Your Word, and fill my mouth with the truth that they need. Remind us as a family to continually commune with You, in Jesus' name. Amen.

Another Good Day

The stone which the builders rejected has become the chief cornerstone. This is from the Lord and is His doing; it is marvelous in our eyes. This is the day which the Lord has brought about; we will rejoice and be glad in it.

PSALM 118:22-24 AMP

If we're honest, we'll admit that not every dawn elicits a smile and a cry of rejoicing from us. Whether we have gotten too little sleep, or we're in pain, or we have a task ahead of us that we'd rather avoid, we are sometimes tempted to think, *Looks like it's going to be another one of those days.*

But we must take issue with that thought. Our expectation determines our attitude, which determines our experience—so if we expect a bad day, then our experience will be bad. The truth is, however, that there are no bad days. No matter what kind of pressure or evil we may face on any particular day, it is not a bad day. God designed it, and He only makes good things.

Today, remember that you live in the day of salvation, the day of grace, the day of provision, the day of healing. You live in the day that was purchased for you two thousand years ago when your God gave His life for your redemption.

The Psalmist prophesied of this day:

The stone which the builders rejected has become the chief cornerstone. This is from the Lord and is His doing; it is marvelous in our eyes. This is the day which the Lord has brought about; we will rejoice and be glad in it.

PSALM 118:22-24 AMP

Jesus was the stone that the builders rejected, the One whose sacrifice purchased this day of God's favor for you. Paul also writes of this day, quoting the prophet Isaiah:

For he says, "In the time of my favor I heard you, and in the day of salvation I helped you." I tell you, now is the time of God's favor, now is the day of salvation.

2 CORINTHIANS 6:2

Every day since the Atonement, Jesus' purchase of our salvation, we have been given a reason to rejoice and be glad. The reason is that today is the day of salvation! The Psalmist gave us a cue for our response to God's provision of this miraculous day when he wrote:

LIVE ON PURPOSE TODAY

No matter what comes your way, remember your Salvation and Redeemer is here for you. Rejoice in Him!

I will confess, praise, and give thanks to You, for You have heard and answered me; and You have become my Salvation and Deliverer.... The Lord is God, Who has shown and given us light [He has illuminated us with grace, freedom, and joy].... You are my God, and I will confess, praise, and give thanks to You; You are my God, I will extol You. O give thanks to the Lord, for He is good; for His mercy and loving-kindness endure forever.

PSALM 118:21,27-29

On this day of grace, freedom, and joy, join with the Psalmist and heaven's choir, praising your Salvation and Deliverer. His mercy and loving-kindness endure forever—they extend even to today. No matter what last night looked like, and regardless of what lies ahead, rejoice in today! What a good gift it is!

PRAYER

Jesus, I praise You, my Salvation and my Redeemer! I will not be downcast; I put my hope in You, my Savior and my God. (Ps. 42:5.) I speak of Your righteousness and my mouth is filled with Your praise, declaring Your splendor all day long. (Ps. 35:28; 71:8.) I will lead my family in boasting of You all day, and we will praise Your name forever. (Ps. 44:8.) In Jesus' name, I rejoice and am glad in this day that You, my Lord, made! Thank You for it, Lord! Amen.

Mints and Other Life Choices

BY MARILYN G. NUTTER

Commit your way to the Lord;
trust in Him and he will do this.

PSALM 37:5 NIV

L eaving the restaurant, we stopped at the candy dish near the door and I took a few of my favorite mints, the pastel-colored ones with the chocolate-flavored peppermint inside. I pass on red and white peppermints and I don't like the white after-dinner mints with jellies inside, but I rarely pass on my favorites. I popped one in my mouth and savored the flavor. Breath mints, peppermints, after-dinner mints, wintergreen mints, extra sweet, slightly tart, or even hot—there are many different mints and each has a unique flavor. Some are used to freshen my mouth after garlic bread and spaghetti, some to "quiet" my tummy after too much food, some to suck on to avoid eating extra calories, and some to chew and swallow to get a little taste of sweetness. Just like candy mints, life offers us many "mint" choices. In adjusting to a new season in life, a new job, or a move, I may encounter all of them, and like the mints at restaurants, I can choose them, avoid them, or savor their flavor.

The one mint that I must have is my appoint*ment*. Keeping an appointment with God on a regular basis is essential to get daily strength, encouragement, and guidance for a decision. As I savor my quiet time, God's encouraging words and promises sweeten my outlook. Keeping my regular appointment with God renews my commitment to Him.

As I listen and learn from Him, I develop security in His plans for me. Keeping my appointment will help me deal with the other "mints" in my life.

Disappointment visits at unexpected times and in different ways. Disappointment with circumstances and people and unmet expectations can be overwhelming, especially when moving or beginning a new job. Dwelling on my disappointments can make me miserable and I fail to see other positive things in life. If I choose to suck on the disappointment, I will miss out what God is trying to teach me.

Contentment can be confusing if I equate it with happiness. "I have learned to be content whatever the circumstances," says the apostle Paul. (Phil. 4:13.)

Happiness is fleeting and depends on happenings. Contentment is joy within and being satisfied with who I am; it allows me to accept my circumstances and other people. An intruder in my life is discontentment, and it surfaces as my critical spirit and unhappiness

LIVE ON PURPOSE TODAY

Determine to have a regular appointment with God. Make a list of the things that bring you contentment and enjoyment. Pray about your disappointments and look for a Scripture that will encourage you.

grow. When I allow discontentment to prevail, I become miserable and pass that on to others.

Enjoyment is pleasant, but I can easily confuse it with entertainment. It may be hard to experience enjoyment if I look for material things and people to provide it for me. Finding joy in the simplicity of life and the gifts it has to offer, appreciating the colorful autumn leaves, a cup of coffee with a friend, an e-mail from 1,000 miles away, a good book, a phone call, and reading a humorous article are simple things that give enjoyment. "God provides everything for our enjoyment." (1 Tim.6:17.)

Restaurants and candy counters offer a wide array of flavors and mint choices. Each day life brings "mint" choices too. I can savor, enjoy, or pass on any of these, but if I want to have peace and security, I'll keep my appointment, and in committing my way to the Lord, I can release my disappointments and savor contentment and enjoyment.

PRAYER

Lord, help me to see the contentment and enjoyment that come from a regular appointment and relationship with You. Teach me Your ways, direct my steps, let Your Word become alive in me. Help me to always be sensitive to what You want to do in my life. As disappointments come my way, help me to give them over to You and trust You. In Jesus' name I pray. Amen.

Hold On Tight

When I found him whom my soul loves;
I held on to him and would not let him go....

SONG OF SOLOMON 3:4 NASB

Do you remember the days of the chase—the days when you first fell in love with your husband? The tingling excitement when you caught his eye from across the room? The first time you held his hand? That momentous first kiss? Now that you've caught this man—the object of your desire—will you hold on to him?

Sometimes the demands of motherhood, and life in general, can distract us from the passion we once felt for our husbands. Our emotional legs can become so tired just from chasing our children that they sometimes fail to carry us to the comfort of our husbands' embrace.

While our children certainly need our loving attention, we must realize that they also need their parents to love each other. When they see a vital relationship between their parents, they feel the stability of a loving home. They see a model of the love God wants them to one day have in marriage. They see the love Christ has for the church. (Eph. 5:22-33.) They gain a strong psychological and spiritual base on which to build their own future.

For the sake of your children, and for the sake of your marriage, remember the chase and hold on to your prize. Once in a while, put down the dishes, the laundry, and even the children to rediscover the man with whom you fell in love. Learn about his interests, and enjoy them with him. Tell him your dreams, and let him help you reach them.

Remember the words of Solomon, who told his son: "...may you rejoice in the wife of your youth" (Prov. 5:18). Rejoice in the husband of your youth. Remember your first days with your husband, and continue to rejoice in him just as you did then.

Years of marriage and parenthood shouldn't diminish the joy you find in your husband. Rather, it should enhance it because you have been given the opportunity to share the life you could only dream of then. Whether your life today is what you imagined or not, don't stop dreaming now. You have a full life of shared opportunities ahead of you. What do you want to accomplish together in that time? In the next year? Today? Commit to staying unified with your husband in every way so that you can accomplish everything for which God united you. Hold on tight. Don't let go.

LIVE ON PURPOSE TODAY

Make an appointment with your husband for some time to focus only on one another.

PRAYER

*Father, thank You for the gift of my husband. I speak blessings
upon him today, in the name of Jesus. Teach me and my husband
how to communicate and meet one another's needs and love
each other more deeply every day. I choose to chase my husband,
just as I did in the days of our youth. I plead the blood of Jesus
over our marriage, and I declare that it is vibrant and strong—
a vivid example for our children to follow in their future marriages.
I am committed to my marriage vows, and I will follow
You in fulfilling them, in Jesus' name. Amen.*

Make an Eternal Impact

No discipline seems pleasant at the time, but painful.
Later on, however, it produces a harvest of righteousness
and peace for those who have been trained by it.

HEBREWS 12:11

Disciplining our children isn't easy, but it is necessary. In order to direct them toward the prosperous and successful lives God wants for them, we will have to make discipline a part of their lives.

Godly parental discipline introduces to children the concept of right and wrong choices, and it steers them toward doing what is right. As we discipline our children, it's important to offer them many opportunities to make good choices. Remember: God empowered Adam and Eve to decide among many good choices when He told them they could eat of any tree in the Garden. Notice, however, that at the same time He empowered them with choice, He clearly identified the boundaries.

"You are free to eat from any tree in the garden; but
you must not eat from the tree of the knowledge of good
and evil, for when you eat of it you will surely die."

GENESIS 2:16,17

God knew it was necessary to set boundaries because He understood the dangers that threatened His creation. He was acquainted with the serpent's rebellious influence, so He gave Adam and Eve a clear directive in order to protect them from harm.

As parents, we know of the dangers that lurk in this world. We're aware of the problems that can result from making bad choices. Therefore, we do what is necessary to protect our children from harm. We offer them good choices, set boundaries, define consequences, and enforce rules, thus giving our children a safe environment in which to grow.

In a nutshell this is discipline, and it is clearly an expression of love. Proverbs 3:12 says, "The Lord disciplines those he loves, as a father the son he delights in." We discipline our children with the intent to keep them safe from harm and to empower them to live the satisfying lives that God intended for them—the lives we want for them because we love them.

LIVE ON PURPOSE TODAY

Write out a discipline plan for your household. Then schedule a family meeting to clearly communicate the plan.

Following God's example, we should always be motivated by love. Love is not bent on self-interest (1 Cor. 13:5), but actively pursues the long-term well-being of others. Because well-being can only be achieved by adherence to God's principles, we must base our parenting structure on His Word.

Proverbs 22:6 NLT says, "Teach your children to choose the right path, and when they are older, they will remain upon it." As soon as our children enter our lives, they need our loving guidance onto the path of God's principles. As they learn to choose that path for themselves, they become a blessing to future generations as well.

God's desire for us as parents is clear:

> Oh, that their hearts would be inclined to fear me and keep all my commands always, so that it might go well with them and their children forever!

DEUTERONOMY 5:29

Today, whether we want to or not, we impact our descendents forever. Whether we intentionally apply that influence or leave the outcome to chance is our choice, but the results will be traced back to our decision. Today, let's accept our responsibility and set our children on a course toward blessing forever.

PRAYER

Father, teach me to lovingly discipline my children. I commit to studying the Bible so that I can direct them on the path that You light with Your Word. Holy Spirit, speak to my heart Your instructions for mothering each of my children. I accept my responsibility to discipline them, and I trust that they and their children will follow You, in Jesus' name. Amen.

Choosing Life

BY ANN PLATZ

> *I have set before you life or death, blessing or curses....*
> *Choose life! ... Cling to the Lord your God, for he is*
> *your life and the length of your days.*
>
> DEUTERONOMY 30:19,20 TLB

With the clock ticking and the world turning ever faster, it seems there is no time—or reason—to bemoan the fact that we are growing older. Statistics show that today we have a larger senior population than ever before. This is the age of longevity. Adults are living longer, taking better care of themselves, and staying active for many more meaningful years. In fact, people age eighty-five and older are the fastest growing segment of society in the United States.

My eighty-six-year-old Aunt Mae Williams, widowed over thirty years ago, is a woman whose passion for life has kept her young. As an artist, she adored her sculpting classes and continued taking them until very recently, when failing eyesight brought that season to an end.

Yet even her limited vision has not dimmed her optimistic outlook. It is her passion for people that has kept her charged with creative energy. This energy, this overflow of her nature, has been essential to her existence. She loves to be around the younger generation, which inspires her to learn and grow, even in the late autumn of her life. Such women are ageless.

Corrie ten Boom, a Dutch Christian, was a survivor of Hitler's death camps. She saw her entire family destroyed, including her beloved sister Betsie, and lived to tell the world that the best is yet to come. How could she have endured such trauma? How could she have traveled the continents as a much older woman, testifying that there is no pit too deep for God to reach, no wound He cannot heal?

As a child, Corrie knew well her earthly father's love. He often tucked her into bed and held his hand against her cheek, murmuring words of love. Remembering the security of his love gave her the courage to offer hope to her fellow prisoners in the Nazi concentration camps. She kept her eyes fastened on the future—not just hope of liberation from the camp, but that eternal hope we have in Christ. She knew that one day all locks would fall away and we would step into eternity with Him, where there is no more weeping, only joy and celebration forevermore.

LIVE ON PURPOSE TODAY

Today, determine to let go of your agenda and take a leap of faith into God's continuing plan for you.

That same security is available to all of God's children. We can march into midlife and beyond with hope and anticipation. We may not all be a Corrie ten Boom; or a Grandma Moses, who first picked up an artist's brush at age sixty; or even an Aunt Mae—but we can face our own future with serenity, look for the possibilities, and listen for the Spirit's leading as we move to the next plateau.

As we leave one familiar season to enter another, God's creativity and bounty are astounding. Our minds and hearts are stretched. Our tents are enlarged, and we are able to have more of Him as we surrender everything we own and everything we are.

The picture of a trapeze artist leaping from one swing to grab another in midair is an image of the faith walk with God. That split-second of releasing the familiar to embrace the new is both exciting and terrifying. What if she should miss the connection? What if she should fall? The Lord designs this move to enhance the believer's intimacy with Him.

The fear of losing present securities is real. To remain locked into old patterns, however, can create legalism and hardened traditionalism. If the Lord is to remodel a home and a heart, a woman must choose to open the door and allow the refreshing Spirit to sweep through.[3]

PRAYER

Father, in Jesus' name, I give You my life. I lay my past at Your feet, and I dedicate my present and future to You. You brought me into this life with a purpose, and I am determined to live each day to fulfill it. Holy Spirit, tell me when to take the next leap. I'm ready to soar with You. Amen.

In His Strength

*But ye shall receive power, after that the Holy Ghost
is come upon you: and ye shall be witnesses unto me
both in Jerusalem, and in all Judaea, and in Samaria,
and unto the uttermost part of the earth.*

ACTS 1:8

Acts 1:8 tells us that when the Holy Spirit comes into our lives, so does His power. That power, called *dunamis* in the original Greek, is "strength, power, ability, inherent power, residing in a thing by virtue of its nature, or which a person or thing exerts and puts forth."[4]

When you welcome the Holy Spirit into your life, you welcome His *strength, power,* and *ability.* The end of Acts 1:8 tells us the purpose of that strength, power, and ability: "...ye shall be witnesses unto me both in Jerusalem, and in all Judaea, and in Samaria, and unto the uttermost part of the earth." *Dunamis* enables us to be witnesses to the world.

As mothers, our greatest influence on the world starts at home. If we want to accomplish great things as mothers, we will need to learn to rely on the strength of the Holy Spirit within. We may be able to do a lot of wonderful things in our own human strength, but not as much as we can in His! At some point the reserves of our human energy and ability will always run out, but God's never will!

When we allow the Holy Spirit to work in and through us, we are no longer limited to the power of the physical body or the physical mind. We rise to a supernatural level of ability and strength—God's ability and strength. In Colossians 1:29 AMP, Paul speaks of this "...superhuman energy which He so mightily enkindles and works within me." As moms, we need superhuman energy—and we can have it every day!

Paul's words to Timothy recorded in 2 Timothy 1:5-7 remind us to live aware of the power of God's Spirit within. We are told that by faith, we lean our entire personality on Him in absolute trust in His power. (See 1 Tim. 1:5 AMP.) We are encouraged "to stir up (rekindle the embers of, fan the flame of, and keep burning) the [gracious] gift of God, [the inner fire]" that is in us (v. 6 AMP). And we are reminded that "[He has given us a spirit] of power and of love and of calm and well-balanced mind and discipline and self-control" (v. 7 AMP).

When we lean our personality on God in Christ by trusting in His power, we are invested with His power, love, and calm and well-balanced mind and discipline and self-control. Imagine how effective we would be as moms if we were to "stir up...the gift of God, [the inner fire]" and demonstrate His character every day!

The way we stir up that inner fire is by spending time in His presence, magnifying

LIVE ON PURPOSE TODAY

Do everything today with God's ability, and give Him the praise.

Him through our words of praise, speaking His words (Scriptures), and praying in the Spirit. Jude tells us that when we pray in the Holy Spirit, we build ourselves up: We "make progress, rise like an edifice higher and higher" (Jude 1:20 AMP). Stirring up the gift of the Holy Spirit within enables us to rise above the challenges of this world. The strength of God's Spirit, this superhuman strength, is what will enable us to be the mothers He has called us to be—to reach our children and this world with His glorious salvation.

PRAYER

Heavenly Father, in the name of Jesus, I praise You! I receive Your gift of the Holy Spirit. I thank You that with Him comes all of Your power, strength, and ability; Your love and Your sound mind. I pray in the Spirit to build myself up. (Jude 1:20.) Thank You, Lord, for ministering through me today. Amen.

When Dad Is Gone

{ *A father of the fatherless, a defender of widows,
is God in His holy habitation.
God sets the solitary in families....*
PSALM 68:5,6 NKJV }

Parenting is a demanding job for anyone, but when a mom is left to care for her children without the support or the presence of their father it can feel like an overwhelming burden. Single moms, God wants you to know that you are not alone in rearing your children. He is with you, and He holds a special place in His heart for your family.

Psalm 68:5 says that God is the father of the fatherless. Your children have a Father—the faithful, loving, powerful, and merciful God. He wants to father them, and He wants you to help them find Him and know Him better every day.

Psalm 68:5 also says that He is the defender of widows. Regardless of the reason for your husband's absence, God wants to be your defender, your protector. In His limitless strength and immeasurable mercy, God will cover You with His wings, where you will find shelter and confidence every day. (Ps. 57:1.) No evil will be able to touch you or your children when you abide in Him, and no sickness or tragedy will be allowed under His covering over you. (Ps. 91:10.)

Psalm 68:6 says that God wants to set the solitary in families. If you feel alone, God sees your need and He wants to fill it. Take every opportunity to surround your family with trustworthy people who are genuinely committed to God and to fulfilling His purpose—and these will become your partners in faith and victory.

The Bible reveals what God can do for your family when you trust Him: "He hath delivered my soul in peace from the battle that was against me: for there were many with me" (Ps. 55:18 KJV). The word "peace" here is the Hebrew word *shalom,* which indicates wholeness—nothing missing or broken. No matter what battles rage against you, God can preserve your wholeness, your children's wholeness, and your wholeness as a family—because He stands with you.

By no means are you or your children alone. Just as a great host of heavenly warriors surrounded Elisha and his servant and protected them from an army of thousands, a great heavenly host surrounds you and your children. (2 Kings 6.) Those who are with you are more than those who oppose you (v. 16)—and God will ensure that you and your children remain whole and victorious through every battle.

LIVE ON PURPOSE TODAY

Meditate on God's ability to protect you and to be a Father to your children. Remind your children of His love today.

Today, trust God to be the Father to your children, to protect you, and to give you a family of faith. Trust Him to meet every need in your lives resulting from the absence of a natural father and husband. Ask Him to reveal Himself so clearly to your children and to you that you live assured of His presence, His protection, His help, and His provision. He wants to meet all of your needs and lead your family into victory, and He will when you trust Him.

PRAYER

Father, before I even speak, You know my thoughts. You know me and You know my children completely. You have seen our needs, and You have provided for every one. I trust You, Lord, because You are altogether trustworthy. I give You my needs and know that You, my defender and protector, will meet each one. I give You my children's needs and know that You, their Father, will meet them. Father, I trust You to lead my family to people who really love You, and who love us as You do. I trust that Your peace will keep each individual in my family whole—nothing missing, nothing broken—and we will live in victory by Your strength every day, in Jesus' name. Amen.

The Gift

BY KAREN R. KILBY

I have loved you, o my people, with an everlasting love;
with loving kindness, I have drawn you to me.

JEREMIAH 31:3

I have heard it said that the best gift a mother could give her children is a positive, loving relationship with her husband. That was not always an easy thing for me—for sure, it did not come naturally.

For the first several years of our marriage, my focus seemed to be on me and what would make me happy. My expectations of a husband and children centered around them meeting my emotional needs and not giving much thought to theirs. It wasn't that David did not try to please me or that my children were not lovable. There just seemed to be a hunger inside of me that could not be satisfied. I would often wonder, *Is this all there is? There must be more to life than this!* The day-to-day tasks of housekeeping and being a loving wife and mother became mundane. *Somehow,* I thought, *I need to find something that will make me feel complete.*

Filling my time with volunteer work, having a part-time job, and moving my family from one home after another as I completed decorating projects, continued to leave me feeling empty and unsatisfied. It was not until a friend shared a book with me called *Peace With God* that I was able to discover the answer.

I learned that before I could begin to understand what a loving relationship could be with my husband and children, I first needed to understand what my relationship needed to be with God. Even though I had grown up attending church, I had never discovered the gift of God's unconditional love that had come wrapped in the Person of His Son, Jesus. As I continued to read the book, I learned that Jesus had come to give me an abundant life, filled with meaning and purpose. (John 10:10.) In turn, I would be capable of passing that gift along to others as Jesus loved them through me. That's what I wanted—a life that counted for something, full of promise and hope. I accepted God's gift for my life, and the emptiness was replaced with contentment and peace. Then I understood, perhaps for the first time, that it was not what David could do for me but what God could do inside my heart.

LIVE ON PURPOSE TODAY

Have you unwrapped God's gift for you today? Have you shared His gift with someone else?

When I began to study the Bible, I learned the love passage that explained what God was teaching me: "Love is patient and kind; never jealous or envious, never boastful or proud, never haughty, selfish or rude. Love does not demand it's own way. It isn't irritable or touchy. It doesn't hold grudges and will hardly even notice when others do it wrong. It is never glad about injustice, but rejoices whenever truth wins out. If you love someone, you will be loyal to him no matter what the cost. You will always believe in him, always expect the best of him, and always stand your ground defending him" (1 Cor. 13:4-8 TLB).

Accepting God's gift was the best decision I have ever made. As God's everlasting love and kindness drew me to Him, it also drew me closer to David and, in turn, closer to my children. Knowing that God's love is focused on me continues to allow me to focus my attention on my family and others.

PRAYER

Thank You, Father, for Your everlasting love that came to earth in the Person of Your Son, Jesus. Let me minister Your love everywhere I go. As I walk in love, people are blessed and lives are changed. Thank You for filling my life with purpose and meaning and enabling me to be an example of Your love to others. In Jesus' name, amen.

Our Children's Faith

Knowing that your faith is alive keeps us alive.

1 THESSALONIANS 3:8 MESSAGE

It's something we'd probably rather not think about—the idea that our children may one day, or may even now, have doubts about the Christian faith. The philosophies of this world lure them every which way but heavenward; and even if we choose to shelter them, our influence can only reach so far.

Our heavenly Father continues to speak to us as He spoke to the Israelites, "This day I call heaven and earth as witnesses against you that I have set before you life and death, blessings and curses. Now choose life, so that you and your children may live" (Deut. 30:19). Because He longs for our blessing and our children's blessing He urges us, "Choose life." Because we take Him at His Word we have chosen life, and because we long for our children's blessing we urge them to do the same.

However, neither God nor we can ultimately choose life for our children. Yes, our choice as moms influences our kids. When we believe God's Word and live what we believe, their lives are absolutely impacted for good. But faith is an action that requires personal choice. Hebrews 11:1 says, "Now faith is being sure of what we hope for and certain of what we do not see." Faith is being sure and being certain. We can't do that for our children. They must do that for themselves.

Certainly, we are not required to sit passively by. In fact, we are commanded to instruct them in the truth all day, every day.

> These commandments that I give you today are to be upon your hearts. Impress them on your children. Talk about them when you sit at home and when you walk along the road, when you lie down and when you get up.

> DEUTERONOMY 6:6,7

By our words and actions, we are to train our children in the way they should go—that is, in the Word of God. Nonetheless, they must ultimately choose God for themselves.

The New Testament apostles lived and died to give people truth. To them true living came when they heard that their teaching had been effective—that the people they had taught continued to choose life. Consider the joy Paul must have felt when he heard from prison "good news about your faith" (v. 6). Suddenly, everything he had suffered became weightless: "For now we really live," he wrote, "since you are standing firm in the Lord" (v. 7).

LIVE ON PURPOSE TODAY

In everything you do and say, encourage your kids to choose life.

Like the New Testament apostles, we want to truly live, knowing our children continue to choose life. Therefore, we must give our children sound instruction; we must give them the Word. Then we must be confident in that Word to work in them, for God has said, "...I send [my word] out, and it always produces fruit. It will accomplish all I want it to, and it will prosper everywhere I send it" (Isa. 55:11 NLT). Speak the Word, live it, pray it, and then trust it to do all that God has sent it forth to do—producing for your children the fruit of eternal life.

PRAYER

Father, thank You for the gift of salvation that You offer my children. You said, "Train a child in the way he should go, and when he is old he will not turn from it" (Prov. 22:6). I dedicate myself to instructing my children every day in the way they should go. In Jesus' name, I ask You to enlighten them and draw them to You by Your Spirit. Thank You, Lord Jesus, that Your sacrifice produces the fruit of eternal life in my children. Amen.

Have a Talk With Dad

Pray like this: Our Father in heaven,
may your name be honored.

MATTHEW 6:9 NLT

Prayer is our connection with our eternal Dad. When Jesus walked the earth, He lived a life of prayer. He took every opportunity to make His way to a place of refuge—a place reserved just for Him and His Dad. Jesus came to the earth to guide and lead others, yet He often slipped away from His closest human companions to recharge and refocus in the presence of His Father.

We, too, are here to guide and lead others—beginning with our children. Just as Jesus took time away from His followers to be replenished in the presence of the Father, so must we. If we want to impact our children for good, we cannot continually pour out of ourselves and never receive from heaven what we and our children so ardently need.

We cannot try to ignore our needs or meet them ourselves, independent of the abundant supply of our Father. When Jesus had a need, He didn't just stifle it or fix it Himself. He was God incarnate, yet He taught us by example how to depend on the Father. When He had a need, He talked to His Father about it. Isn't it good to know that we, too, can talk with our heavenly Father—the Creator of life, our provider, our unlimited source of wisdom and counsel—and receive all that we need?

Not only did Jesus exemplify a life of prayer, but He also taught us how to pray. Prayer is an immense privilege and responsibility that we as believers must not take for granted, and we must teach our children from an early age that they, too, can have a real connection with their heavenly Dad through prayer. When they need counsel, healing, favor, or provision, they can go to their heavenly Dad, who willingly gives them every good gift when they ask. (James 1:17.)

Prayer is our opportunity to communicate with our all-powerful Dad, and His power effects change in our world through the words we speak. Jesus taught us the power of the prayer of faith when He said, "Have faith in God....if anyone says to this mountain, 'Go, throw yourself into the sea,' and does not doubt in his heart but believes that what he says will happen, it will be done for him" (Mark 11:22,23). Natural circumstances must submit to the spoken Word of God. Isaiah 55:11 CEV says, "...my words...don't return to me without doing everything I send them to do." When natural circumstances oppose supernatural truth, we have the privilege and the responsibility to speak God's Word over them and watch them change to reflect God's will on earth as it is in heaven.

LIVE ON PURPOSE TODAY

Talk to the Father throughout your day— and include your children at every opportunity.

Let's follow Jesus' example and spend time with our heavenly Dad so that we can know and do and speak His will on the earth, and so that we can teach our children to do the same.

PRAYER

*Father, I love speaking with You. You are everything I need, and
I rest in You now. Teach Me Your will so I can do what You want me
to do and speak what You want me to speak so that Your will is done
here on earth—in my life, in my home, and everywhere I go in
prayer—as it is in heaven. Teach me and my children to depend
on You daily for everything we need, in Jesus' name. Amen.*

The Weapon That Conquers Fear

There is no fear in love. But perfect love drives out fear....

1 JOHN 4:18

God's will is for us to have an abundant life. Jesus said, "The thief does not come except to steal, and to kill, and to destroy. I have come that they may have life, and that they may have it more abundantly" (John 10:10 NKJV). The enemy comes to steal, kill, and destroy us, and his ultimate target is our faith because our faith overcomes every weapon he has formed against us:

> For whatever is born of God overcomes the world.
> And this is the victory that has overcome the world—our
> faith. Who is he who overcomes the world, but he who
> believes that Jesus is the Son of God?
>
> 1 JOHN 5:4,5 NKJV

Because the devil so longs to conquer our faith, he has developed a tool that has disarmed people of every age, race, and gender. That tool is fear.

Second Timothy tells us that "God has not given us a spirit of fear, but of power and of love and of a sound mind." Fear is a spirit, and it is not a gift from God. It is a weapon sent against us from the enemy. James 4:7 says, "Submit yourselves, then, to God. Resist the devil, and he will flee from you." When we resist the demonic spirit of fear, it has to flee!

In opposition to the fear that the devil tries to defeat us with, God has given us a spirit of "power, love, and a sound mind." That Spirit is the Holy Spirit, and He resides within us and has given us all of His attributes. We have His power. Jesus promised we would: "...you will receive power when the Holy Spirit comes on you..." (Acts 1:8 NKJV). We have His love: "Whoever lives in love lives in God, and God in him" (1 John 4:16 NKJV). We have His sound mind: "We have the mind of Christ" (1 Cor. 2:16 NKJV).

First John 4:18 focuses on one of these attributes as the invincible weapon against fear. It says, "There is no fear in love. But perfect love drives out fear...." Ten verses before, in 1 John 4:8, we read that God is love. In order to conquer fear in our lives, we need true love: God Himself.

LIVE ON PURPOSE TODAY

Get to know God. Get to know love. Then get ready to overcome everything that stands against Him, in Jesus' name.

In both 1 John 4 and 1 Corinthians 13, the word translated "love" is the Greek word *agape*, which refers to God's love. First Corinthians 13 gives us a definition of love and, therefore, a concise description of God. A deeper look at this definition helps us to better understand this weapon that will always conquer fear.

Perhaps the chapter's final description of love, found in 1 Corinthians 13:8, illustrates its power best: "Love never fails." According to *Thayer's Greek-English Lexicon of the New Testament*, this means that love never "fall[s] overcome by terror or astonishment or grief or under the attack of an evil spirit or of falling dead suddenly." It is never "cast down from a state of prosperity [or] uprightness." It never "perish[es], i.e come[s] to an end, disappear[s], cease[s]. It never "lose[s] authority, no longer hav[ing] force." It is never "removed from power by death."[5] Love never, ever stops under any condition whatsoever. It always was, always is, and always will be. It is completely unchanging and unconquerable, because it is God Himself.

This love, this powerful force that cannot be stopped, is the weapon that always conquers fear, and it resides in us because God's Spirit resides in us. When the spirit of fear tries to enter our homes, we can kick it out in the name of Jesus. If we will continually invite into our homes the presence of Love Himself, Jesus Christ, we will be able to watch every fear melt away.

PRAYER

Father, in Jesus' name, I thank You for the opportunity to know You through Your Son. You are love, and nothing can stand against You. In Jesus' name, and by the power of His blood, I resist the spirit of fear that would try to come against me or my family members. Holy Spirit, I welcome You and thank You that You fill each of us with Your power, love, and sound mind every day. Amen.

The Hard Way

BY TRACIE HUNSBERGER

*But if we confess our sins to him, he is faithful and
just to forgive us and to cleanse us from every wrong.*
1 JOHN 1:9 NLT

I dropped out of school at 15. I was so busy trying to grow up that I never thought about the fact that I wouldn't know what to do when I finally got there. I had my son one month after my eighteenth birthday, not yet married and without any education. I looked into his eyes. He was six pounds and helpless without me. I began to wonder what his life would be like. Would he struggle the way that I had? What did I have to offer him?

I knew it would be hard to go back to school with a child, but what would happen to him if I didn't? When I looked into his eyes, I wanted to see a shining future full of every opportunity I could give him. I knew to get there I would have to work hard and set my sights high. He was my treasure. He was my reminder that each generation has a choice to define their destiny.

I went back to high school and graduated. Then I went on to college. I'm married now and have four great kids. I learned a lot the hard way and I don't recommend it, but I know that no matter what is in our past, we have a choice every day to either become what God has planned for us, or just to let another day slip by. When God looks at us He feels the same way I do when I look

LIVE ON PURPOSE TODAY

Maybe you have made some mistakes, but God wants to forgive you. Decide to make a fresh start today. God's mercy is here for you and His destiny is waiting for you.

into my son's eyes. He knows the great things we can achieve if given the opportunity, He does everything He can to make our choice easy, and then He leaves the choice up to us.

PRAYER

Father God, I'm sorry. Forgive me. Thank You for making me clean. Help me to start fresh. Help me to fulfill my destiny in You, in Jesus' name. Amen.

Becoming Spirit-Minded

So we make it our goal to please him, whether
we are at home in the body or away from it.

2 CORINTHIANS 5:9

We live in a very physically minded world. The media portrays men and women in top physical condition. Many teens and adults, trying to attain the same image, struggle with eating disorders or look to plastic surgeons to try to salvage their poor self-image.

As believers we know that physicality is not the most important aspect of our lives. In fact, among the three parts of the human being—spirit, soul, and body—the body is arguably the least important because it depends on each of the other two parts to function. Knowing this, we need to focus on our spirits more than we focus on our bodies. Our children need to see us properly valuing each part of our being.

When we focus on the spirit, we gain a proper perspective of the body. The human body is the Master's design, and it truly is a masterpiece. Psalm 139:14 says, "I praise you because I am fearfully and wonderfully made; your works are wonderful." Beauty is truly in the eye of the beholder, and when God beholds each one of His creation He sees flawless beauty. This perspective is what should shape our own and our children's body image.

We cannot neglect the spirit, but neither can we neglect the body. The health of the body is essential to attaining the long, satisfying lives on earth that God desires for us. The Psalms attest to this desire of our Father: "With long life will I satisfy him and show him my salvation" (Ps. 91:16). Therefore, maintaining our physical health through exercise, nutrition, and rest is working hand-in-hand with God toward the fulfillment of His desire. Note, however, that God promises this long, satisfied life to a specific kind of person: one who "loves me" and "acknowledges my name" (v. 14). The life of the spirit plays a vital role in the quality of the life of the body.

Our goal as parents should be to teach our children to live by the spirit. When they live motivated by the spirit, they will not be flesh-driven. In a time when the flesh is glorified above the spirit, we would do well to direct our children's focus back to what really matters.

This focus-shift must begin with our dedication to making the spirit within us the director of our lives. The apostle Paul wrote, "We make it our goal to please him, whether we are at home in the body or away from it" (2 Cor. 5:9). When our spirit directs our body's actions, we please the Father.

LIVE ON PURPOSE TODAY

How can you strengthen each part of your being today—spirit, soul, and body?

The writings of Paul offer us another focus-shifting message about the body: "Do you not know that your body is a temple of the Holy Spirit, who is in you, whom you have received from God? You are not your own" (1 Cor. 6:19). We are not our own! Our body is important because it is a vehicle by which the Holy Spirit moves in the earth today. Our determined purpose should be to use the body God has given us for His glory.

Give your children a strong example of one who glorifies Him in body so that they will see the good fruit of a spirit-driven life.

PRAYER

Father, in Jesus' name, I pray that You'll give me Your perspective on the three parts of my being. Teach me to properly edify each part of me and of my children. I pray that You'll help me and my children have a self image that completely reflects Your image of us, in Jesus' name. Amen.

Pockets of Peace

BY ANN PLATZ

He calls his own sheep by name and leads them out.
After he has gathered his own flock, he walks ahead of them,
and they follow him because they recognize his voice.

JOHN 10:3,4 NLT

L istening involves finding quiet times and places to hear God's voice; to receive advice, information, and wisdom; and to release joy and freedom. The Good Shepherd promises that His sheep will know His voice and that He will lead them to green pastures. The decision for the believer is whether she will allow the voice of the Shepherd to be heard over the babble of her world.

Younger people don't understand the need for quiet moments in a noisy world. While they search for excitement, older people crave stillness. It is all about taking a break, about relaxing and breathing deeply, about savoring the stuff of life.

You don't have to build a cabin in the mountains to find peace and quiet. Anyone can locate a space—large or small, elaborate or simple—to prop her elbows on a windowsill of heaven and gaze into the face of the Father. Whatever the place, it should be yours alone, dedicated to your moments with the Master. It can be a special desk or a cozy window seat, a favorite tree or a bench in the garden. You can find it anywhere—and when you do, you'll wonder why it took you so long to get there.

A gracious hostess has the ability to elicit conversation from her guests. She will initiate a topic, then ask others to interact. When you go to God in these moments of reflection, you may bring up the topic, but don't monopolize the conversation. Wait for His response. Bask in His presence. Enjoy Him.

Listen actively—with the desire to learn and with the intent of sharing.[6]

LIVE ON PURPOSE TODAY

Commit your attention
to the Good Shepherd,
and learn to recognize
His voice.

PRAYER

Father, I need Your wisdom so desperately. I repent for allowing other noises to distract me from Your voice, which gives me perfect direction and peace. I want to know Your voice so well that no other sound can confuse me or lead me astray, so I dedicate my time and my attention to You. Speak to me, Lord. My heart is listening. In Jesus' name, I pray. Amen.

Open the Door

*He will turn the hearts of the fathers to their children,
and the hearts of the children to their fathers....*

MALACHI 4:6

Your children need your wisdom. They need your guidance. They need your heart. God has a special purpose for each of your children, and He chose you to be a guide for them along their path to reaching the full potential He has placed within them. Everything about you—everything you have become and everything He has equipped you to be—can benefit your children. But the door of communication must be open between you and your children in order for these gifts to be passed from you to them.

Not only do you have gifts to give them, but they have gifts to give you. When you train them in the Bible and when they have the Spirit of God residing within, your children become mouthpieces of God's wisdom. Don't close the door on that possibility, and don't be afraid to speak God's wisdom into them.

Don't allow fear or pride or anything else to barricade the door of communication between you and your children. God wants to deliver many gifts to you and to your children through that door. He wants to give you a whole relationship with each other, and He wants to reflect His glory through you to each other.

> And all of us have had that veil removed so that we
> can be mirrors that brightly reflect the glory of the Lord.
> And as the Spirit of the Lord works within us, we become
> more and more like him and reflect his glory even more.

2 CORINTHIANS 3:18 NLT

The state of the family is becoming increasingly significant. Malachi 4:5-6 prophesied:

> "See, I will send you the prophet Elijah before that
> great and dreadful day of the Lord comes. He will turn the
> hearts of the fathers to their children, and the hearts of the
> children to their fathers; or else I will come and strike the
> land with a curse."

Luke 1:17 tells us that John the Baptist went "on before the Lord, in the spirit and power of Elijah, to turn the hearts of the fathers to their children and the disobedient to the wisdom of the right-eous—to make ready a people prepared for the Lord." He prepared the hearts of the people for Christ's coming by minis-tering to unite families.

LIVE ON PURPOSE TODAY

With a hug, a note,
or a word, open the
door of communication
with each of your
children today.

Christ is coming again, and to be prepared our hearts need to be toward each other in the home. The Father's desire is harmony in the home, and He requires that it be found according to His Word. Children are to "obey" their "parents in the Lord," meaning parents are to regulate their children's lives by God's Word. (Eph. 6:1 NKJV.) Parents are not to "provoke [their] children to wrath, but bring them up in the training and admonition of the Lord" (v. 4 NKJV). In short, God's way is the only way to have true harmony in the home.

Open the door of communication between yourself and your children by opening the door to God's Word in your family. God waits for the door to open so that He can bless your home. Break down the barriers, and get ready to give and receive all the gifts God has for your family.

PRAYER

Father, thank You for the gift of my children. I pray that You'll help me communicate to them in a way that will open doors, rather than shutting them. Teach me by Your Spirit how to effectively communicate Your Word and will to them so that they have a peaceful life. Thank You for a peaceful, harmonious home. I will obey Your Word and teach my children in Your ways, and their peace will be great, in Jesus' name. Amen.

Provision for Your Family

I was young and now I am old, yet I have never seen
the righteous forsaken or their children begging bread.
They are always generous and lend freely;
their children will be blessed.

PSALM 37:25,26

God is, has always been, and will always be the best financier. He wants us and our children to be secure in Him so that He can make our finances secure. Matthew 6:33 KJV says, "But seek ye first the kingdom of God, and his righteousness; and all these things shall be added unto you." When His kingdom is our focus, He provides everything we need on earth.

The primary financial principle we'll learn from God's Word is that of sowing and reaping. When we sow, we reap. In other words, when we give something of our substance (a seed), we receive multiplied times what we have sown (a harvest). Second Corinthians 9:11 shows us God's intention toward those who give of their substance:

> You will be made rich in every way so that you can be generous on every occasion, and through us your generosity will result in thanksgiving to God.

2 CORINTHIANS 9:11

This is what God wants to do through and for us and our families. He wants to give us everything we need and more so that we can give to those around us in need.

It starts with our willingness to part with the seed that is already in our hands. It may not look like much, but in God's economy that "little" seed can multiply and become more than enough to provide for our families and bless the people around us.

God sees our need, and He sees our children's needs, and He will always provide for them when we trust Him. The Psalmist wrote:

> I was young and now I am old, yet I have never seen
> the righteous forsaken or their children begging bread.
> They are always generous and lend freely; their children
> will be blessed.

PSALM 37:25,26

LIVE ON PURPOSE TODAY

Plant a seed.
Then thank God for
the harvest—in the
recipient's life and in yours.

God has provided all that we and our families need to live an abundant life. God doesn't want us to lack any good thing. (Psalm 84:11.) When we look at our children, we must remember that they are first and foremost their heavenly Father's. We must allow Him to take full responsibility for them by surrendering them to Him in prayer. Amazingly enough, He wants (and is able) to take care of them more than we do (and can)!

God has given us and our families the key to unlock His storehouse of provision. It is His Word. When we read it, believe it, speak it, and live it, we will see His blessings poured out on our families. We will see that God is everything He promised He would be—when we take Him at His Word.

PRAYER

Father, in Jesus' name, I seek Your kingdom today. As I look in Your Word, I see that it is Your will to provide for my family. I recognize the seeds You have placed in our hands, and I thank You that as we plant them they become a bountiful harvest for us to enjoy and to give. I am a cheerful giver, Father, and I am glad to be Your blessed daughter! Amen.

Stay Open

BY JULIE LECHLIDER

"My thoughts are completely different from yours,"
says the Lord. "And my ways are far beyond anything
you could imagine. For just as the heavens are higher
than the earth, so are my ways higher than your ways
and my thoughts higher than your thoughts."

ISAIAH 55:8,9 NLT

After two and a half years, Scott and I were excited to be moving back to our hometown with our young family. However, the house we moved into was quite a bit more expensive than the house we had moved from, so it was certain that I would have to return to work.

One cold December morning, after I saw my husband off to work, one daughter off to school, and the other down for her morning nap, I sat down in front of the crackling fireplace with my yellow highlighter to wade my way through the classified ads, looking for a new career. After a long morning of dead-end phone calls, I was beginning to get frustrated. The phone rang and I answered it, hoping it was someone calling to set up an interview, but it was only my uncle who had just called to chat. My uncle was not walking with God and wasn't really open to hearing about the gospel, so I did not expect him to give me any real encouragement. After I explained what I was doing, he suggested that I contact a company I had worked for before we moved. I was strongly opposed to it—I had been there and done that and was ready for something new. However, after I hung up the phone the words kept coming back to me—the feeling just wouldn't go away. Later that afternoon, I decided to call an old friend that was still employed there just to see how things were going. After we talked for a few minutes and I told her that I was job hunting, she exclaimed that she had just been talking about me that same day because they were looking for someone to fill my old position and she had heard that I was back in town. By the end of that week I had been hired, and I was offered more money than I actually needed to make!

That was nearly four years ago, and today I know deep in my heart that God called me to the position I now hold at the company. I love what I do, and I have flexible work hours that allow me to be home for my daughters after school and to take care of my family. I have the best of both worlds. It scares me to think where I might be today had I not obeyed what God was telling me to do—and He gave me direction through the most unlikely person.

LIVE ON PURPOSE TODAY

God works in ways
we do not expect—
so stay open. Trust God,
no matter how unusual
His ways look.

PRAYER

Father God, in Jesus' name, I am going to stay open to Your ways. I receive Your wisdom over my own ideas. I welcome You to work in my life. Amen.

No Shame

The two of them, the Man and his Wife,
were naked, but they felt no shame.

GENESIS 2:25 MESSAGE

In the Garden of Eden before sin entered the world, man and woman lived together "without shame." Eve, the first woman, respected herself and her husband. Adam, the first man, respected himself and his wife.

God made Adam in a specific way, and He formed Eve in another specific way. However, despite their differences, man and woman were completely comfortable in one another's presence. Neither felt shame in self, and neither felt shame in the other.

According to God's design, man and woman walked openly together without shame. However, the moment sin entered the world, that mutual respect was lost.

At that moment, their eyes were opened, and they suddenly felt shame at their nakedness.

GENESIS 3:7 NLT

The Bible calls Satan our accuser. (See Rev. 12:10.) When Adam and Eve believed his lie and sinned, they welcomed his accusations into their lives. In their fallen state, Adam and Eve felt shame in themselves and in one another. Adam, confronted with his sin, complained about his wife: "It was the woman you gave me..." (Gen. 3:12 NLT). Feeling the sting of shame within, he became a spokesperson for the accuser. Eve followed: "The serpent tricked me.... That's why I ate it."

Since that time, the enemy has continued to whisper accusations inside of people, and many have unsuspectingly become his voice against themselves and others. Everything from one's physical appearance to one's personality, under his condemning scrutiny, becomes a source of shame. What results is disrespect for God's creation and, ultimately, for God Himself.

It was for this reason that Jesus came:

> For God did not send his Son into the world to condemn the world, but to save the world through him.
>
> JOHN 3:17

Isaiah, prophesying of Jesus, wrote:

> Because the Sovereign Lord helps me [Jesus], I will not be disgraced. Therefore have I set my face like flint, and I know I will not be put to shame. He who vindicates me is near. Who then will bring charges against me? Let us face each other! Who is my accuser? Let him confront me!
>
> ISAIAH 50:7,8

At the Cross, Jesus confronted our accuser and His. He confronted Satan, and He overcame him! Colossians 2:15 says, "Having disarmed principalities and powers, He made a public spectacle of them, triumphing over them in it."

Isaiah's prophecy concludes:

> This is what you [the devil and his demonic forces] shall receive from my hand: You will lie down in torment.

> ISAIAH 50:11

The book of Revelation confirms the ultimate destiny for our accuser:

> Then I heard a loud voice in heaven say: "Now have come the salvation and the power and the kingdom of our God, and the authority of his Christ. For the accuser of our brothers, who accuses them before our God day and night, has been hurled down."

> REVELATION 12:10

Today, the accuser is defeated. He has no power in the lives of those who have accepted Jesus as Lord and walk in His authority. Still he has yet to be "hurled down." This will occur after Jesus' return. For this reason, 1 Peter 5:8 warns, "Be sober, be vigilant; your adversary the devil walks about like a roaring lion, seeking whom he may devour."

LIVE ON PURPOSE TODAY

Ask your family members to forgive you for words you have spoken against them. Speak words of victory over each one today.

The devil would love to devour us and everyone around us. When we listen to his accusations about parts of our lives, we give him those parts to devour. When we speak his accusations against others, we allow him to devour them through us. What a contradiction to the victory Jesus won for all of us! We must be vigilant against the devil's accusations, which cause us to tear down self, others, and ultimately God.

Satan is defeated, and we must rise with Christ above his accusations.

> Therefore we were buried with Him through baptism into death, that just as Christ was raised from the dead by the glory of the Father, even so we also should walk in newness of life.
>
> ROMANS 6:4

We must not remain in spiritual death, allowing the devil's accusations to come out of our mouths in attack on ourselves or others. We must become a voice for our victorious Lord, proclaiming with Him, "Because the Sovereign Lord helps me, I will not be disgraced. Therefore have I set my face like flint, and I know I will not be put to shame." Today, let us become a voice for salvation and illuminate Christ's victory in every life we reach.

PRAYER

Father, in Jesus' name, I praise You. You are wonderful, and Your works are wonderful. Thank You for sending Jesus to defeat our accuser. I ask You to forgive me for ever siding with him against Your creation or against You. I dedicate to speaking Your words of victory over all people, and words of praise to You, in Jesus' name. Amen.

Out of the Mouth of Babes

*Out of the mouth of babes and nursing infants
You have ordained strength, because of Your enemies,
that You may silence the enemy and the avenger.*

PSALM 8:2 NKJV

The Bible lists many reasons to pray, and one of them is to silence the voice of the enemy.

First Peter 5:8-9 says,

> Your enemy the devil prowls around like a roaring lion looking for someone to devour. Resist him, standing firm in the faith....

As believers, we have the authority to resist the enemy through prayer in the name of Jesus. That power is not limited to adult believers. In heavenly society, there is no differentiation between people of varying age. Psalm 8:2 NKJV says, "Out of the mouth of babes and nursing infants You have ordained strength, because of Your enemies, that You may silence the enemy and the avenger." According to God's plan, children have the strength in their mouths to silence the enemy.

In Matthew 21, the prophecy of Psalm 8:2 is fulfilled:

> When the chief priests and the teachers of the law saw the wonderful things he did and the children shouting

in the temple area, "Hosanna to the Son of David," they were indignant.

"Do you hear what these children are saying?" they asked him.

"Yes," replied Jesus, "have you never read, 'From the lips of children and infants you have ordained praise'?"

MATTHEW 21:15,16

The enemy will always try to silence praise of the Most High God, but the strength in the mouths of God's children invariably silences the enemy.

LIVE ON PURPOSE TODAY

Teach your children about their God-given authority.

As a mother, you have the privilege of instructing your children to use the strength God has given them to stop the enemy's attempts to avert the plan of God. That strength within your children will grow as you empower them with instruction from the Word of God of their rights as believers.

Your example will be the best teaching tool as you instruct your kids in their authority over the enemy. When he tries to enter your home with sickness, depression, or any of his weapons of darkness, resist him in the name of Jesus. You don't have to shout or put on a show; simply stand in your authority—and watch him flee.

Submit yourselves, then, to God. Resist the devil, and he will flee from you.

JAMES 4:7

The devil trembles when he sees children of God who know their rights—whether those children are three or ninety-three. By your example and your instruction, lead your children into an understanding of their rights as sons and daughters of God.

PRAYER

Father, thank You for the authority You have given Your children in the name of Jesus. Through Your Word and by Your Spirit, teach me and my family to use our voices to silence the voice of the enemy in the authority of Jesus' name. We exalt You in our home and in our lives, and no work of the enemy can stand against the greater One in us, in Jesus' name. Amen.

Your Personal Spring

*"...whoever drinks the water I give him will never thirst.
Indeed, the water I give him will become in him
a spring of water welling up to eternal life."*

JOHN 4:13,14

One day on His way from Judea to Galilee, Jesus passed through a town called Sychar in Samaria. In Sychar, He saw Jacob's well and, tired from the journey, He sat down to rest beside it. As He rested, a Samaritan woman came to draw water from the well. Seeing that this man was Jewish, she must have bowed her head uncomfortably, drawn the water quickly, and expected to quietly depart with her brimming bucket. However, a parched voice broke through her silence, asking, "Will you give me a drink?" (v. 7).

Having experienced years of strict segregation from the Jews, this woman must have been completely taken aback. "You are a Jew and I am a Samaritan woman," she said. *Perhaps he didn't realize,* she might have reasoned. "How can you ask me for a drink?" (v. 7).

Jesus' voice had broken into this woman's God-silent world, and it was about to change her life. "If you knew the gift of God and who it is that asks you for a drink," He said, "you would have asked him and he would have given you living water" (v. 10). He continued:

"Everyone who drinks this water will be thirsty again, but whoever drinks the water I give him will never thirst. Indeed, the water I give him will become in him a spring of water welling up to eternal life."

JOHN 4:13,14

Jesus offered this woman living water that would quench her every thirst. She was thirsty for a relationship with God, but she had been trying to satisfy that thirst with human relationships. Addressing her misplaced energies, He said, "...you have had five husbands, and the man you now have is not your husband..." (v. 17). Suddenly the woman knew He was a prophet, and later she even said, "I know that Messiah...is coming. When he comes, he will explain everything to us." Jesus said, "I who speak am he" (v. 26).

Jesus identified Himself as the Messiah, and the woman dared to believe. When she returned home, she couldn't help but tell all of her friends about this amazing Man, saying, "He told me everything I ever did" (v. 39). As a result of her testimony, many came to Jesus, listened to His words, believed—and received the living water that never runs dry.

LIVE ON PURPOSE TODAY

Spend time in God's presence, and let His living water satisfy every need in your life.

Jesus offers you that same living water today. Will you accept His offer? If you have received Jesus, the Messiah, in your life, He has become within you a spring of water that wells up every moment of your earthly life and continues to well up to eternal life. You don't have to wait to experience the goodness of God that certainly awaits you in heaven. You can experience it now.

Drink deeply of Jesus today. He satisfies. In truth, He is the only satisfaction you will ever know. You can't be satisfied with a drink or with human relationships or with anything else on earth, but only with the living water that Jesus is in you today.

Isaiah prophesied:

> Therefore you will joyously draw water from the springs of salvation.... Praise the Lord in song, for He has done excellent things...for great in your midst is the Holy One of Israel.
>
> ISAIAH 12:3,6

Today, praise the Lord for being your living water. Praise Him for being your satisfaction, your provision, your hope, your Lord, your Savior—anything and everything you need, for He truly is all you will ever need.

PRAYER

Father, in Jesus' name, I drink deeply of the living water You are in me. Jesus, let Your spring of salvation bubble over in me, touching everyone around me with Your supernatural substance that satisfies, heals, and saves. I praise You, Lord, for meeting all my needs, and those of my family and friends and all whom I meet. Amen.

The Power of Friendship

Holy Father, keep them and care for them—all those you have given me—so that they will be united just as we are.

JOHN 17:11

D o you remember when you entered the league of mothers—the day you held your child in your arms for the very first time? Suddenly you were a part of a society that perhaps you never realized existed. You personally discovered a whole new series of experiences and emotions that countless women throughout history understood, but that had been completely foreign to you until that moment. You realized how much you needed the guidance and, especially, the friendship of other mothers.

Mary and Elizabeth shared the extraordinary bond of motherhood. When Mary became pregnant with Jesus by the Holy Spirit, she went immediately to stay with her cousin Elizabeth, who was pregnant with John the Baptist at the time. As soon as Elizabeth heard Mary's voice, her child leaped in her womb. There was a deep connection in the spirit realm between these two mothers and their two children. The Holy Spirit spoke through Mary and Elizabeth, and they rejoiced together over the fulfilling of God's eternal plan of redemption in and through them and their children. (Luke 1:39-56.)

God desires to give us friendships like that of Elizabeth and Mary. He wants mothers to be a refuge for one another to turn to in time of need and in time of rejoicing. He wants us to be able to speak freely to one another under the anointing of the Holy Spirit. He wants us to be able to lift up His name and rejoice together over the fulfilling of His plan in each other's lives and the lives of our children.

God wants us to have the support and advice of godly friends. Proverbs 12:26 says, "The godly give good advice to their friends...." We can trust God to lead us to godly friends who will give us good advice, and He will. When He does, we will need to remember that good advice is not always what we want to hear. Sometimes it can be painful because it pulls us out of our comfort zones. Sometimes it stings, but we need to remember that "wounds from a friend can be trusted, but an enemy multiplies kisses" (Prov. 27:6).

LIVE ON PURPOSE TODAY

Reach someone with Jesus' friendship today.

Above all, we need to remember that we have a friend whose love will never fail us. John 15:13 says, "Greater love has no one than this, that he lay down his life for his friends." Jesus wants our friendship more than anything—so much that He gave His life to us to attain it. He will be there for us through every situation—when your children try our patience or when they are far from home; when our human friends are distant, geographically or emotionally; when human companionship is nowhere to be found. He is there for us, and when we draw close to Him He will draw close to us. (James 4:8.) As we do, He will teach us how to be godly friends and He will draw godly friends into our lives. He will restore our present relationships and bring new ones to us.

Thousands of years ago, Jesus spoke a prayer for us that is still in effect today because His words go forth to accomplish His pleasure. (Isa. 55:11.) He said, "Holy Father, keep them and care for them—all those you have given me—so that they will be united just as we are" (John 17:11 NLT). Jesus longs for us to be united with believers who will encourage us and support us through every season of life. When we trust Jesus, the friend who sticks closer than a brother (Prov. 18:24), He will bring us all the friendship we will ever need.

PRAYER

Father, I draw close to You, and I thank You for drawing close to me and drawing friends to me. I dedicate myself to being a godly friend who willingly gives and receives godly advice, rejoices over the fulfilling of Your will in others' lives, and always supports others in prayer and love. Lord, I pray that You would change lives through me as I willingly reach out to others with Your friendship, in Jesus' name. Amen.

A Woman Who Listened

BY ANN PLATZ

{ *"Speak, for your servant is listening."*
1 SAMUEL 3:10 NIV }

During my career, I have often been invited to speak at design seminars and conferences. In addition, I lead a group of Christian women in retreat settings from time to time. All this involves a lot of talking. But I'd rather be remembered as a woman who listens.

Mary, the mother of Jesus, revealed a listening heart when the angel of the Lord appeared to her, bringing a prophecy. When she was told that she would be the mother of the Messiah, she did not resist or offer excuses. Instead she replied, "I am the Lord's servant, and I am willing to do whatever he wants. May everything you said come true" (Luke 1:38 TLB). Later, when visiting with her cousin Elizabeth, Mary praised the Lord for showing favor to her.

As in any conversation, both speaker and listener were crucial. Mary's response to the word of the Lord was first obedience, then praise and adoration. She knew that all generations would call her blessed because the Mighty One had done great things in her.

For the remainder of her earthly life, she was quick to hear and obey. At God's prompting, Mary and Joseph moved to Egypt to protect the Gift entrusted to them. Later they were instructed to return to Nazareth to bring up the Child. Here in their care, Jesus "increased in wisdom and stature, and in favor with God and men" (Luke 2:52 NKJV).

Perhaps Jesus learned some of His listening skills from His godly mother. He, too, listened for His Father's voice and did what He saw His Father doing. (See John 14:10 TLB.) His life's purpose was to hear and obey instantly.

When Mary stood at the scene of the crucifixion on that dreadful day, she heard her Son, the incarnate God, speak from the cross to her and then to His beloved disciple John, "He is your son...she is your mother" (John 19:26,27 TLB). How His loving words must have comforted Mary as He released her into His friend's keeping.

Mary's heart was quiet. Therefore, she was able to hear and receive some of the greatest messages ever delivered. Through her all generations of the world have, indeed, been blessed.

LIVE ON PURPOSE TODAY

Offer God a listening heart, and discover true rest and life-changing revelation in Him.

I pray that you and I can find the green pastures and still waters of our lives long enough to be still and know God more intimately. Let's agree to listen more and speak less. Let's carve out quiet places in our homes and our hearts for renewal and rest.

Jesus knows your name. Be still and listen. He is calling....[7]

PRAYER

*Jesus, I quiet my mind right now. I make myself still in
Your presence so that I can know You more intimately.
Speak to me, Lord; Your servant is listening. Amen.*

The Rose Tree

BY NANCY B. GIBBS

*Then God saw everything that He had made,
and indeed it was very good.*

GENESIS 1:31 NKJV

I'll never forget the day that I was greeted by dozens of blooming red roses. The rose tree was one of the most beautiful gifts that God has ever given to me.

Immediately after we moved into our home, we planted a running miniature rose bush beside the driveway. Since it didn't have anything to climb on, it simply rested on the ground as the bush grew longer and longer. To our surprise one spring day, we noticed a seedling pine growing near the bush. Another pine tree was the last thing we needed, but we didn't have the heart to pull it up.

"God planted it," we reasoned, "so it would stay there." We didn't know what a gift of beauty that God had in store for us. As the little tree grew, the rose bush clung to its branches. It wrapped its stems carefully around every limb and reached for the sky. It seemed that the rosebush grew much faster after the seedling appeared. Like people, it needed something to hold on to. Together the tree and rosebush grew until one day the buds on the rosebush blossomed and filled my yard with beauty and splendor. It was a sight to behold—one that I will never forget.

Children are much like that rosebush. Physically, they will grow in stature, but it takes love and happiness for them to grow in spirit. They desperately need caring parents to lean on and the love of Jesus to cling to. In a world where crime is rampant and violence is growing among our young people, the gospel of Jesus Christ is more crucial than ever before. By shutting God out of their lives, we are asking for trouble for our children. By allowing Him to govern their lives, they will thrive, while growing stronger and more beautiful with each passing day.

God faithfully stands near His children just as the pine tree stood beside the little rosebush. We have a choice to make. Will we teach our children to reach out to Him, depending on Him for all of their needs, or will we allow them to face the world alone? The world is a frightening place.

Giving our children the roots which they need can only serve to make them more beautiful, as they grow stronger in the Spirit of the Lord. With God to hold on to, every child has the potential to bloom where they are planted.

LIVE ON PURPOSE TODAY

When we teach our children to cling to the love of God, we are giving them something that they cannot find anywhere else. God's roots are deep and His love is strong. Won't you entrust your children to Him today?

PRAYER

Dear God, thank You for being with my children as they struggle to find their places in this world. Reveal to them the desires and plans that You have for them. Fulfill Your plans and purposes in their lives. Lord, help me to glorify You in my role as a mother and to know when to hold on and when to give them roots and let them go. In Jesus' name I pray. Amen.

Precious in His Sight

*"Can a mother forget the baby at her breast and
have no compassion on the child she has borne?
Though she may forget, I will not forget you!"*

ISAIAH 49:15

D o you recall the day you brought your child home for the
first time? The joy and the anxiety of calling this perfect
being your own? Deep inside you felt the weight of value
God placed on this child, and you wanted to become the best
parent you ever thought you could be so you could give this child
more than you ever had.

Whether that day in your life was yesterday or ten years ago,
God wants you to know that He still holds your child close to His
heart. With one glimpse of His Son, you can see His passion for
each one. Indeed, He sent Jesus as the primary spokesperson of
His love and honor for them.

Consider the message He gives us through the Gospel accounts.

In Matthew 18:3-6, He acknowledges children's matchless
ability to believe in Him and pronounces harsh judgment on any
who would deter them from walking with Him:

> Truly I say to you, unless you are converted and
> become like children, you will not enter the kingdom of
> heaven. "Whoever then humbles himself as this child, he is

the greatest in the kingdom of heaven. And whoever
receives one such child in My name receives Me; but
whoever causes one of these little ones who believe in Me to
stumble, it would be better for him to have a heavy mill-
stone hung around his neck, and to be drowned in the depth
of the sea."

MATTHEW 18:3-6 NASB

In Matthew 18:10, He speaks of the continual attentiveness
of God and His angels to the well-being of children. His statement
is a warning to any who would harm them, yet an encouragement
to any who pursue their welfare.

Take heed that ye despise not one of these little ones;
for I say unto you, That in heaven their angels do always
behold the face of my Father which is in heaven.

In Matthew 19:13-
15, He welcomes the little
children and lays His
hands on them:

LIVE ON PURPOSE TODAY

**Remind your kids how
precious they are
to God—and to you.**

Then some
children were brought
to Him so that He
might lay His hands
on them and pray; and
the disciples rebuked
them. But Jesus said, "Let the children alone, and do not
hinder them from coming to Me; for the kingdom of heaven
belongs to such as these. When he had placed his hands on
them, he went on from there."

With His welcome, Jesus succinctly conveys God's value for these young ones; and with His blessing, He administers the power of God to them to pursue Him all of their days.

Today, we are privileged to bring our children to Jesus so that they can know Him, believe in Him, and receive His blessing and anointing in their lives. We have the responsibility to live right before them and before the God who is continually watching over them. And we have the mandate to esteem them, for they are precious in His sight.

PRAYER

Father, words can't express my gratitude for the children You've given me. I highly prize the gift of each one, and I wholly accept the responsibility of nurturing them as a representative of You. Jesus, love my children through me. Father, thank You for sending Your angels to guard them today and every day. Holy Spirit, direct them on the path of righteousness for Your name's sake. Lord, I praise You for Your continual work in my children and in me, in Jesus' name. Amen.

Continual Praise

*And each morning and evening they stood before
the Lord to sing songs of thanks and praise to him.*

1 CHRONICLES 23:30 NLT

Nearing the end of his reign as king of Israel, David prepared all of the building materials his son Solomon would need for the construction of the Temple. Then he gave assignments to the descendents of Levi for service in the temple. Among them was the mandate to give thanks and praise to the Lord each morning and evening.

Today we, too, have an important responsibility. The Bible tells us that by His sacrifice on the cross, Jesus made us kings and priests (Rev. 1:6; 5:10), and our "body is the temple of the Holy Ghost..." (1 Cor. 6:19). As priests in our individual temples, we need to thank and praise God every day.

David's instruction to the Levites was to thank and praise the Lord twice daily—at the beginning and at the end of each day. Taking it even further, Paul wrote that we should "always give thanks for everything to God the Father in the name of our Lord Jesus Christ" (Eph. 5:20 NLT). As believers, we can thank and praise God all day long, every day!

Not only is it important for us to fulfill the personal assignment of continual thanksgiving and praise, but as mothers we have another vital assignment. The Bible says, "A wise woman builds her house..." (Prov. 14:1 NLT). Just as David provided the building materials for the construction of the temple, we can provide for our children the building materials for the construction of their lives upon the foundation of the Word of God. Then, like David, we can assign them the task of daily praise and thanksgiving.

As God-appointed leaders in our homes, our first action in incorporating praise is to practice it ourselves. Remember: King David didn't just tell the Levites to do it; He equipped them with the instruments for the task. (1 Chron. 23:5.) Furthermore, he had lived it himself since his days in the sheep fields.

As mothers, we need to equip our children with instruments to praise God: our example of a life of praise and tools for worshipful expression. If they are musically gifted, we can equip them with musical instruments. If they are artistic, we can give them paints and canvases or pens and paper. If they love nature, we can provide instruments for them to see and study the wonders of God's creation. Most importantly, we can support them as they use their voices to verbally express thanks and praise to God—every day.

LIVE ON PURPOSE TODAY

Along with each of your children, list at least three reasons you are thankful to God today.

PRAYER

Lord, I thank You and praise You today for Your presence in my life and my children's lives. I am so thankful to know You, and I want my family to praise You every day. Help me openly express my thanks to You in front of my children, so that they will become increasingly comfortable with expressing their thanks and praise to You, in Jesus' name. Amen.

Sex Education

{

*For this reason a man will leave his father and mother
and be united to his wife, and they will become one flesh.*

GENESIS 2:24

}

God made man and woman sexual creatures. He gave each of us the anatomy to reproduce, as well as the capacity to enjoy sexual pleasure. Sex is a beautiful gift from God and, just as with every other gift He has given us, He wants us to enjoy it.

As we rear our children, we are faced with some important questions on this topic: *When do we teach our kids about sex? And How much do we say?*

The fact is that we live in a society that bombards our kids with sexual images every day. Whether we choose to teach them about sex or not, they will learn. The question is what do we want them to learn—or, better still, what does God want them to learn?

Starting at birth, our children can be given a healthy, scriptural look at the beautiful gift of sexuality. The first thing we can teach them is that God created them, male and female, and each is a wonderful creation. As they continue to grow, they will need to learn God's parameters for sex, which are first mentioned in the first book of the Bible:

For this reason a man will leave his father and mother
and be united to his wife, and they will become one flesh.

GENESIS 2:24

A man is to be united to his wife and to become one flesh
with her. Notice: marriage comes first, uniting comes second, and
finally the two become one flesh. The phrase "one flesh" indicates
not only the sexual unity between the two but also the unbreak-
able bond between their persons resulting from the sex act. In
God's eyes, they become one. In the parameters of marriage, this
is a beautiful image; but outside of it, it becomes the image of
bondage and imprisonment.

While today's public sex education proliferates the idea that
pregnancy and sexually transmitted diseases are the worst possible
consequences of premari-
tal sex, the truth is that
the act itself can injure
lives. Sex can attach
people who would not
otherwise have become
attached; and when they
separate, they lose a piece
of themselves forever.

LIVE ON PURPOSE TODAY

**Look for opportunities
to share with your kids
God's perspective
of sexuality.**

Without a full-life
commitment, sex can
destroy not only a couple
but their two individual lives. Some may argue that a full-life
commitment can happen without a marriage. However, the
covenant of marriage is a clear indication to both a man and a
woman that each is committed to the other for life. Without it,

one or the other must deal with the fear that the union between them—and, therefore, they themselves—will be broken.

While the consequences of premarital sex are dismal, the rewards of sex in marriage are beautiful. Children need to know that sex is a wonderful, God-given experience to be shared between a man and a woman who have committed their entire lives (not just their bodies) to one another. They need to know that sex is only worthwhile when it is shared between a man and a woman who want to remain united for life and have demonstrated that desire in the covenant of marriage—and then it is a precious gift to both.

PRAYER

Father, I pray that You'll help me to speak honestly with my children about Your gift of sexuality. Help me not to shy away from teaching them the truth. I pray that You would open up the lines of communication between my kids and me so that I can share Your truth with them and encourage them to wait for Your best for them—a loving marriage relationship. Lord, give my kids the courage and the wisdom to protect their virginity until they are united in marriage, and then reward them with a joyful relationship, in Jesus' name. Amen.

Ruining the Feast

BY SUE ANNE ALLEN

{ *Better a dry crust with peace and quiet than
a house full of feasting with strife.*

PROVERBS 17:1 }

My energy dips as I descend the valley of late afternoon. By this time of day, my disturbed sleep and my laundry list of daily responsibilities begin taking their toll. My body is ready for a nap, but I am the housekeeper, I am the carpool driver, I am the snack getter-outer, I am the homework helper, I am the piano assistant, and I am the dinner cook. My identity at 4:00 P.M. each day can be summed up in three tiny letters: M-O-M. M-O-M could easily be translated: "no nap for the weary."

So, instead of a nap, I say a prayer on this blank journal page, asking, Lord, that You empower me to be the M-O-M my family desperately needs. Give me enough rest in these moments of meditation to be rejuvenated as I care for my family's natural needs. May You adorn my heart with peace and my face with a genuine smile.

I relate to Proverbs 17:1 at 4:00 o'clock in the afternoon. "Better a dry crust with peace and quiet than a house full of feasting with strife." Lord, help me to remember that my attitude is of utmost importance. My rage ruins a feast. When I slam the juice cup in front of my 3-year-old after he has relentlessly repeated, "Mommy, can you get me more juice?", when my 7-year-old looks up at me with her big blue eyes, asking for help on her first grade homework, and I snap "Can't you just do it yourself?", and when I yell at the top of my lungs, "Turn that music down!" when my other kids are dancing freely in the middle of the living room to their favorite CD, I ruin our afternoon feast.

At 4:00 P.M. I am a tired juggler, but my exhaustion must not turn into resentment toward my needy children. I do not want to serve up strife with their afternoon snack. Instead, my exhaustion must turn into moments of prayerful recharging if my children are to experience the taste of God's gentle Spirit in our home each day. Your love, Your joy, Your peace, Your patience, Your kindness, Your goodness, Your self-control, Your faithfulness, and Your gentleness welling up from within me will bless even a crust that is a little too dry. My kids will not remember the sensation of dryness as they chew, but they will unconsciously record the peace or the strife that accompanies the food my hand extends to them.

LIVE ON PURPOSE TODAY

Remember that God has promised to fill you to overflowing with the fruits of His Holy Spirit. Sit quietly in His presence. Receive, with gratitude, His abundance.

PRAYER

Bless me, Lord. Bless me with the fruits of Your Spirit. Help me to trust You and to know that You have everything under control.

Help me to stay steady and not overreact to people or situations but to be patient in all things. When life is hectic, demanding, and busy, help me to not let frustration and anxiety steal patience out of my heart. Pour Yourself into my heart so that I have sweet refreshment to serve my hungry children. In Jesus' name, amen.

Reclaim Your Emotions

For all who are led by the Spirit
of God are children of God.

ROMANS 8:14 NLT

Have you ever felt as if your emotions were completely out of your control? Perhaps something aggravated you, and your feelings just took over. Your heart raced, your face flushed, your fists clenched, and your mouth started verbally expelling whatever ugly emotion you were feeling. At one time or another—or perhaps on a fairly regular basis—each of us has allowed emotions to take control.

Emotions are a part of the human experience, and they aren't essentially bad. In fact, emotions are immeasurably beneficial to us. Some of them help us enjoy our daily experiences, and some of them help us avoid danger. Emotions often serve us well. However, when emotions take control of our actions, they can cause major problems for us and for the people around us.

The apostle Paul tells us in the book of Galatians that if we live in the spirit, we will not gratify the lusts of the flesh. (Gal. 5:16.) Our flesh has a good time running free with emotions; however, it is not always beneficial to us or to the people around us to give our emotions that control. It might feel good to let anger loose with a pound of the fist or a verbal assault, or to let self-pity express itself with tears and complaints; however, acting on those negative feelings doesn't help anyone. In fact, it often hurts others—and it always hurts us.

Many of us have felt the ongoing tremor of bitterness even after we've cried and complained in self-pity. We have felt the floods of guilt when we've acted out in anger. We have discovered for ourselves how destructive our emotions can be when they take control, and we know that we shouldn't allow them to do so. What we need to know, though, is that we can reclaim control over them.

The wonderful thing about knowing God is that He offers us a solution for every difficulty we face. For the difficult task of controlling our emotions, He offers us the power of His indwelling Spirit to take back the reigns and restore peace to our souls.

Some of the desires of the sinful nature listed in Galatians 5 are "hostility, quarreling, jealousy, outbursts of anger, selfish ambition...envy..." (Gal. 5:19-21 NLT). Each of these desires is equally destructive when acted upon, but each can be overcome by the same power—before they become actions. It doesn't matter whether you are struggling with feelings of hostility, jealousy, or anger: God offers you the power to control every feeling by the power of His Spirit.

The key is to act in His power. Romans 8:13 NLT says, "But if through the power of the Holy Spirit you turn from [the sinful nature] and its evil

LIVE ON PURPOSE TODAY

Submit your emotions to the power of God's Spirit and His Word.

deeds, you will live." When we "keep in step with the Spirit" (Gal. 5:25), we overcome the impulses of destructive emotions.

We don't have to be overcome by emotions. We can overcome them! When we choose to allow God's indwelling power to motivate our actions, we will display His nature: "love, joy, peace, patience, kindness, goodness, faithfulness, gentleness and self-control" (Gal. 5:22,23). Then we will demonstrate whose we are, "for all who are led by the Spirit of God are children of God" (Rom. 8:14 NLT).

When we feel weak, and our emotions feel strong, we can lean on God's grace that is sufficient for us. (2 Cor. 12:9.) In our weakness, God's power will enable us to reclaim control over our emotions and produce the good fruit of His Spirit.

PRAYER

Father, in Jesus' name, I thank You for the power You have imparted to me in the Person of the Holy Spirit. In Jesus' name, and by Your power, I take control of my emotions, thoughts, and actions and submit them to You. Your Word tells me to rejoice in You always, so I rejoice in You always! (Phil. 4:4.) Thank You for Your power working in and through me, producing the fruits of Your Spirit, in Jesus' name. Amen.

Good Friends for Your Kids

I am a friend to all who fear you,
to all who follow your precepts.

PSALM 119:63

C hildren need friends. In truth, we all do. Friends pick us up when we fall, and they rejoice when we rise. Good friends play, laugh, cry, and pray together, and they provide each other with a tangible image of Jesus' love:

> Greater love has no one than this, that he lay down
> his life for his friends.... I have called you friends....

JOHN 15:13,15

While the company of friends brightens our lives, "bad company corrupts good character" (1 Cor. 15:33). The character of our friends makes a vital impact on our character. As mothers we may train our children in God's ways, but the friends they choose will deeply affect their long-term commitment to that training.

For this reason, part of the training we give our children must address the importance of choosing good friends. Throughout our children's time at home, we can help them with the task of making good relationship choices. We should be well acquainted with our children's friends, as well as their friends' families. We should be observant of our children's behavior both when they are with their friends and afterward. Most importantly, we should lean on the wisdom of the Holy Spirit. If our hearts tell us something is wrong with a relationship in our child's life, whether we have a logical reason or not, we need to heed the Holy Spirit's voice. He knows so much better than we do, and His wisdom will keep our children safe from every kind of harm.

The Bible is packed with examples of good friendships that we can introduce to our children when they are very young and remind them of often as they grow. Our children will be encouraged to see the results of bonding with people of good character as seen in the lives of such biblical characters as David and Jonathan (1 Sam. 18-23; 2 Sam. 1-21); Daniel, Shadrach, Meshach, and Abednego (Dan. 3); Mary and Elizabeth (Luke 1); Jesus, Mary, Martha, and Lazarus (Luke 10:38-42; 16); and the first members of the New Testament church (Acts 1).

As we teach our children about choosing friends, we need to remind them especially of the example of Jesus, who reached the lost through friendliness (Mark 2:17; Luke 7:34) and offered His friendship to those who followed God's commands (John 15:14). Our kids' closest friends should be those who follow God's commands. When they are with acquaintances who do not, they need to remember to be leaders and not followers—and we should be diligent to help them make the distinction.

The most important thing we can do to help

LIVE ON PURPOSE TODAY

Talk with your children about the importance of choosing good friends and being a good influence.

our children make the right choices in friendship is to ensure their friendship with Jesus.

> God...invited you into this wonderful friendship with
> his Son, Jesus Christ our Lord.
>
> 1 CORINTHIANS 1:9

When our kids know Him personally, and when they seek Him for themselves, they will make good choices in all of their human relationships—and their closest Friend will be glorified because of it.

PRAYER

Father, I ask You to send good friends to each of my children.
Holy Spirit, guide me and each of my kids in our spirits
as my children build friendships. Help my children to discern
between good and bad company, and help them influence others
with Your Word and Your love, in Jesus' name. Amen.

A Mother's Spiritual Care

> *And my God shall supply all your need according*
> *to His riches in glory by Christ Jesus.*
>
> PHILIPPIANS 4:19 NKJV

T he ability to care for our children's physical needs comes instinctively to us. As new mothers, we quickly learned how to feed, clothe, bathe, shelter, and provide a restful environment for our babies. However, along with these physical needs, our children also have similar spiritual needs—and God has supplied them all.

For example, we bathe our children regularly with the resources we have to keep their bodies clean—water, soap, and wash cloths. Likewise, we need to bathe them regularly with the resources God has provided to keep them spiritually clean. Ephesians 5:25-27 tells us what those resources are: "...Christ loved the church and gave himself up for her to make her holy, cleansing her by the washing with water through the word, and to present her to himself as a radiant church, without stain or wrinkle or any other blemish, but holy and blameless." In order to bathe our children spiritually, we need to introduce them to Christ and His Word, which will cleanse their hearts and keep them spiritually pure.

As another example, we feed our children daily what they need for a healthy physical life. Likewise, we need to nurture their spiritual health daily. Jesus told us just what they need in their spiritual diet: "I am the bread of life. He who comes to me will never go hungry, and he who believes in me will never be thirsty" (John 6:35). We need to regularly feed our children the words and the power of Jesus, for He is the bread of life that will satisfy their every need.

Furthermore, we provide physical shelter for our children to live in, safe from the elements and dangers outside. In the spiritual realm, also, we must lead our children to shelter. The Psalmist spoke of this spiritual shelter: "For You have been a shelter for me, a strong tower from the enemy. I will abide in Your tabernacle forever; I will trust in the shelter of Your wings" (Ps. 61:3,4 NKJV). The heavenly Father is our shelter. Beginning when they are in the womb, we can speak to our children of their eternal shelter in their Father's loving arms.

We also provide an environment to encourage our children to rest their bodies as they need to. Likewise, we need to provide an environment conducive to their spiritual rest. Psalm 46:10 says, "Be still, and know that I am God." We need to teach our children that true spiritual rest occurs regardless of the surrounding circumstances—that it comes from being still and knowing God is in control and will always keep them safe and victorious.

LIVE ON PURPOSE TODAY

Nurture your children's spirits today.

God knows our children's needs, and He wants to become their sole source of supply. As you lead your children to Him, pray and trust that they will learn to lean increasingly on Him to meet all of their needs—physical, emotional, and spiritual.

In order to properly care for the spirits of the children God has placed in your care, you will need to replenish your own. Remember the One who has promised to meet all of your needs, and run to Him daily. His supply is more than enough!

PRAYER

Father, I commit to replenish my spirit in the Word and in You every day. I want to properly nurture my children's spirits. Help me to give them all they need by giving them You. In Jesus' name I pray. Amen.

Family

BY ANN PLATZ

God setteth the solitary in families.

PSALM 68:6 KJV

Barbara Bush, the wife of the former president of the United States, captivated the entire country in her well-publicized address at the Wellesley College commencement when she said: "At the end of your life, you will never regret not having passed one more test, not winning one more verdict, or not closing one more deal. You will regret time not spent with a husband, a friend, a child, or a parent."

The family is God's original institution for communicating His love. The ideal of a loving husband and wife with children, grandchildren, and great-grandchildren is the medium for the message. The message itself is simple: Love God with all of your heart, soul, mind, and strength, and love your neighbor as yourself.

Who is your neighbor? Neighboring starts at home. Generally, the people who share your house—your family—are your original neighbors.

A loving, well-functioning family models God's relationship with His body—the church. Respect for individual members and for authority, forgiveness, patience, encouragement, and praise flow freely in a household consecrated to the Lord.

LIVE ON PURPOSE TODAY

Take every opportunity
to express God's love to
your family today.

The order of the family—the husband and father as head—is important. This is God's chain of command, His plan for the protection of the wife and children. Submission is not a matter of yielding one's personal authority as a woman, but accepting God's wise provision for protection.

The greatest challenge for the maturing woman who understands and accepts this concept may lie in loving her family with agape love—that unconditional, no-strings-attached kind of love with which God loves us. As our birth families become spiritual families, the curse will be reversed; the broken-hearted will be healed; captives will be set free; and garments of praise will replace mantles of mourning.[8]

PRAYER

Father, thank You for the gift of my family. I am grateful for each member, and I commit to offering them the love You have given me. Thank You for the protection You offer me through my husband. Holy Spirit, strengthen and bless him. Help me to be an encouragement and blessing to him, as well as to my children, in Jesus' name. Amen.

Rejoice Over Your Children

The Lord your God...will take great delight
in you, he will quiet you with his love,
he will rejoice over you with singing.

ZEPHANIAH 3:17

I n the Bible, we find God repeatedly approving of His children. Perhaps the most memorable account of God's verbal approval occurs at His Son's baptism. Matthew 3:17 says, "And a voice from heaven said, 'This is my Son, whom I love; with him I am well pleased.'" At that moment, God publicly honored His Son.

As mothers, we have the precious opportunity to speak approval into the lives of our children—to praise them, just as God praises us. (Zeph. 3:17.) Admittedly, at times it seems there is little in our children to praise, but must it be any different for our heavenly Father with us? Not one of is without sin (Rom. 3:23), yet God rejoices over us.

Zephaniah 3:15 says, "The Lord has taken away your punishment, he has turned back your enemy." Eternal redemption has come to all of us through Jesus' sacrifice on the cross, and when we receive it we are no longer subject to the punishment our former sins deserved. We are not spiritual slaves or orphans. Rather, we are children of God.

For [the Spirit which] you have now received [is] not
a spirit of slavery to put you once more in bondage to fear,

but you have received the Spirit of adoption [the Spirit producing sonship] in [the bliss of] which we cry, Abba (Father)! Father!

ROMANS 8:15 AMP

As our Father, God gives us assignments and has high expectations of us. He knows that through Christ, we can do all things (Phil. 4:13), and He always sends us out on assignment with a word of approval. For example, when He sent Gideon into battle against all odds, He said, "The Lord is with you, mighty warrior" (Judges 6:12). When He called Saul, He explained, "This man is my chosen instrument to carry my name before the Gentiles and their kings and before the people of Israel" (Acts 9:15).

In each case, God named the person what He needed him to be so he could fulfill His plan. He pronounced Gideon a "mighty warrior," and Saul His "chosen instrument." In context, we know that neither man appeared to be what God was calling him. Gideon was self-described as the least in the weakest clan (Judges 6:15), and Saul had recently been "breathing out murderous threats against the Lord's disciples" (Acts 9:1). Yet both men became exactly what God had called them.

LIVE ON PURPOSE TODAY

Speak acceptance, approval, and faith-filled words over each of your children today.

In the same way, we can speak words of encouragement, approval, and faith over our children so that they can

{ 126 }

fulfill their God-given assignments. We can speak positive words over their spiritual condition, their behavior, their academic efforts, and everything about them.

As we speak words of faith over our children in their hearing, we fill them with the confidence and faith to become what we have said. Today, let's have faith in our children. Let's speak words of encouragement over them. Let's spend time rejoicing over them—just as their heavenly Father does. Then let's watch them rise in His strength to meet His expectation and fulfill His calling.

PRAYER

Lord, thank You for the opportunity to give my children the priceless gift of confidence in You and Your ability to work through them. I dedicate to speak faith-filled words of praise over them. Help me reflect Your heart for them every day, in Jesus' name. Amen.

Release the Burdens

If your life feels heavy today, God wants to help you get rid of the burden. Isaiah prophesied, "For You shall break the yoke of their burden and the staff on their shoulders, the rod of their oppressor..." (Isa. 9:4 NASB). Verse 6 describes how the yoke of burden would be broken: "For a child will be born to us, a son will be given to us; and the government will rest on His shoulders..." (v. 6 NASB).

The child Jesus, born in Bethlehem, fulfilled this prophecy and broke the yoke of burden that once rested on our shoulders. A yoke is "a curved piece of wood...fitted on the neck of oxen for the purpose of binding to them the traces by which they might draw the plough."[9] Ever since the fall of man, the devil had bound an invisible yoke around every human neck so that we could haul every kind of spiritual, mental, and physical destruction. When Jesus sacrificed His life and became sin for us, He removed that yoke.

When we become Christians, we lay down the burden and accept His proposal:

> "Come to me, all you who are weary and burdened, and I will give you rest. Take my yoke upon you and learn

from me, for I am gentle and humble in heart, and you will
find rest for your souls. For my yoke is easy and my burden
is light."

MATTHEW 11:28-30

Jesus offered us His yoke and burden, the easy yoke and
light burden of His Word, in exchange for the painful yoke and
heavy burden of sin. Yes, the requirements of His Word are a yoke
and a burden—and we feel their weight if we try to perform them
in our own strength. But 1 John 5:3-5 says, "...his commands are
not burdensome, for everyone born of God overcomes the world.
This is the victory that has overcome the world, even our faith.
Who is it that overcomes the world? Only he who believes that
Jesus is the Son of God."

Though His commands are a burden—or a responsibility—
they are not burdensome because of our faith in Jesus. Jesus
wants us to walk yoked to
Him the rest of our days
so that we can perform
God's will not in our own
strength but in His.
Because of His sacrifice,
the burdens of sin and its
resulting destruction no
longer belong to us. If we
are carrying those old
burdens today, it is not
because they haven't been
removed. It is because we
have run back to the
place of our liberation—

LIVE ON PURPOSE TODAY

**Drop the burden of
the past, take on Jesus'
easy yoke and light burden,
and accomplish His will
in His strength.**

the Cross—picked up the burdens, and put them back on our ourselves to carry in our own strength.

Jesus wants us to be free. Galatians 5:1 says, "It is for freedom that Christ has set us free. Stand firm, then, and do not let yourselves be burdened again by a yoke of slavery." In order to walk in the freedom that Jesus eagerly desired and won for us, we have to set down the weight of the past, as Hebrews 12:1-2 NLT says:

> ...let us strip off every weight that slows us down, especially the sin that so easily hinders our progress. And let us run with endurance the race that God has set before us. We do this by keeping our eyes on Jesus, on whom our faith depends from start to finish.

No runner wins a race when she's looking at the starting line. She must look to the finish. We look to the finish by keeping our eyes on Jesus. (v. 4.) If we want to win this race to which God has called us, we must let go of the burden of the past, accept Jesus' offer to shoulder the weight of the yoke and burden of His call, and keep looking to Him. We began this journey of faith in Him, and we will finish it in His strength.

PRAYER

Jesus, I look to You, the author and finisher of my faith. I cast my cares on You because You care for me and You can bear every one with Your strength. I rest in You and win with You, Lord. Amen.

You Can't Have a Testimony Without a Test

BY KATHY PRIDE

Blessed is the man who perseveres under trial, because when he has stood the test, he will receive the crown of life that God has promised to those who love him.

JAMES 1:2

I couldn't believe it. There I was in baggage claim in the Los Angeles airport having a conversation with Mr. T. You know, the Mr. T., from *Rocky*.

Believe it or not, I didn't know who he was at first. We were flying from Philadelphia to Los Angeles and were sitting in the Philadelphia airport waiting to board our flight. My husband leaned over and gave me a nudge. "Look over there. Do you recognize that guy?" Just by the way he said it I knew I should but I was coming up short. Even the heavy gold chain with a large spoon dangling around his neck didn't give it away.

Other clues didn't register either. Converse sneakers, a patriotic T-shirt, and a couple of autograph seekers should have clued me in. One was even bobbing up and down sparring an imaginary opponent. My husband, exasperated by my lack of recognition, clued me in with an audible sigh, complete with rolling eyes and one of those "I really don't believe you" looks.

Rocky, you know, the movie? You know, Mr. T.? And if you don't remember that, ask him if he has spoken to ALF lately. That was it! I knew he had looked familiar....

I missed my autograph opportunity while we were waiting in Philly, but I saw him again by baggage claim in L.A. where he remained unnoticed.

Well, I thought, *it's now or never,* so I rummaged through my purse searching for something he could autograph. The only thing I could come up with was the book I had just purchased in the airport bookstore entitled *Praying Like Jesus.*

Not being shy about my faith, I approached him, book in hand. There I was face to face with Mr. T.

I introduced myself and asked if he would autograph my book. Given the title he replied he would be honored. Before doing so he reached down and pulled out a well-worn copy of a Bible. He tenderly cradled the Book in his hands, telling me he always traveled with his favorite Book. He continued speaking, telling me about service work he had just completed. He told me that when he traveled, he made it a point always to incorporate some type of giving back, and had distributed clothing at a homeless shelter earlier that day. As for the jewelry, he said it always served him well as a conversation piece.

LIVE ON PURPOSE TODAY

Open your heart to the wonderful, creative ways of our Creator and the lessons He has for us.

He autographed the book for my son Matt, asking about him. Matt had just completed a nine-week therapeutic wilderness program to deal with substance abuse and had spent two additional months at a program in New Mexico, and would be returning home the following week. He looked at me with a gentle smile and said, "You know, my mama always used to say, you can't have a testimony without a test...no sir, got to have that test to have a testimony." We shook hands and our eyes communicated a shared understanding.

God introduced me to Mr. T that day to remind me of an important truth. It is often through life's hardships and struggles that our testimony to God's faithfulness develops.

PRAYER

*Lord, thank You for being such a creative teacher. I never cease
to be amazed at how You grab opportunities to teach Your truths.
May we always be open to the lessons You have for us, no matter how
unusual the classroom or the teacher. In Jesus' name I pray. Amen.*

A Lifetime of Honor

*But if a widow has children or grandchildren, these should
learn first of all to put their religion into practice by caring
for their own family and so repaying their parents
and grandparents, for this is pleasing to God.*

1 TIMOTHY 5:4

During the formation of the New Testament church, the
believers were given specific instructions for caring for
the people in need among them. In a letter to Timothy,
the apostle Paul thoroughly outlined the church's responsibility
for widows. The young widows were instructed to remarry and
care for their families, and the elderly ones (over 60 years) were
entrusted to their children's and grandchildren's care. The remaining
elderly widows were supported by the church, and those who
met certain qualifications became part of the ministerial team of
the church and were compensated as such. (1 Tim. 5:9,10,17.)[10]
The elder men of the church were also compensated for their work
in the church. (1 Tim. 5:17.)

Today, many people lean on the government to support the
elderly among them. However, as God's children, we are called to
honor our fathers and mothers. This honor doesn't end when we
move out of our parents' homes. It continues throughout our
entire lives.

One day Jesus rebuked the Pharisees and teachers of the law
for misleading their followers in this regard. He said:

"God said, 'Honor your father and mother' and
'Anyone who curses his father or mother must be put to
death.' But you say that if a man says to his father or
mother, 'Whatever help you might otherwise have received
from me is a gift devoted to God,' he is not to 'honor his
father' with it."

MATTHEW 15:4-6

With these words, Jesus revealed to us that a sign of honoring our parents is our supporting them throughout our adulthood. He also revealed that when we fail to help them when it is in our power to do so, we are cursing them.

The word *honor* in this verse means "to estimate, fix the value; to revere, venerate."[11] How we care for our parents demonstrates how much we value them and their God-given position in our lives. Whether we've had good or bad experiences with them, we must honor them not according to those experiences or our feelings but according to the Word of God.

When our parents become dependent on others for care, we must be the first at their sides to offer our support. We need to find out what our parents need from us and do all in our power to help them. When we honor our parents in this way, God will honor us and help us meet the task. If we ask Him to, He will

LIVE ON PURPOSE TODAY

With your husband,
pray for your parents
and his. Find a way to
honor them today.

give us the wisdom, the courage, and the resources to follow His
Word by honoring our parents as He wants us to all of our days.

PRAYER

*Father, I choose to obey Your Word by honoring my
parents and my husband's parents. I pray that You would
give my husband and me the wisdom to honor them as
You want us to, the courage to stand beside them in their
times of need, and the resources to care for them when they
need us to. Lord, thank You for being our parents' provider, healer,
and friend. Use us to bless them today, in Jesus' name. Amen.*

Training Future Husbands and Wives

For this reason a man will leave his father and mother and be united to his wife, and they will become one flesh.

GENESIS 2:24

A s moms, we have a lot to think about every day. We make sure our kids are bathed, fed, educated, entertained, disciplined, and more. However, as we train them, how often do we look ahead through the years to the time when our sons will be husbands and our daughters will be wives?

The way we rear our kids greatly influences the way they will one day treat their spouses. Consider conflict resolution, for example. Our kids notice every day how we treat our husbands and how we allow them to treat us and each other. They watch, they listen, and they learn.

Our homes are the best environment for our children to learn the necessary skills for resolving conflict. Proverbs 17:17 NKJV says, "...a brother is born for adversity." Sibling rivalry is a common factor in every family, and as moms we are responsible to help our children peacefully settle their disputes so that they'll become masters at the crucial skill of conflict resolution. Our example as wives, as well as our instruction as moms, gives our children a clear picture to look to as they grow.

As we teach our children necessary life skills, we must remain conscious of our example. We need to consistently take responsibility for our actions and do all that we can to maintain peace in each of our relationships. Hebrews 12:18 NKJV says, "If it is possible, as much as depends on you, live peaceably with all men." Although we can't control whether others choose to live peaceably with us, much depends on us.

To maintain peace with our family members, we have to overcome one immense impediment—the reluctance to say "I'm sorry." As moms, and as wives, we must become more interested in doing what's right than in being right in our own minds. If we make a mistake or if we hurt someone, we need to acknowledge what we've done—whether or not we, too, have been wronged.

Rather than ruminating over our injuries, we need to ask God and our loved one to forgive us for the pain we have inflicted and seek restoration—as quickly as possible.

Ephesians 4:26 instructs us: "Do not let the sun go down while you are still angry." When we wait to resolve conflict, we allow ourselves, our loved one, and our relationship to remain broken. Resolution restores wholeness. The sooner it occurs, the better.

LIVE ON PURPOSE TODAY

Help your children work on one characteristic that will help them be good spouses.

Today, let's use our example and our influence wisely as our children grow into men and women. Let's keep in mind our future sons- and daughters-in-law and train our children to be a blessing to them.

PRAYER

Father, I pray for my children's future spouses. Lord,
I want to bless them by training my children to love them,
respect them, and live peacefully with them. Help me give
them a good example to look to as they build their own
lives and marriages, in Jesus' name. Amen.

God's Word on Health

{ *Dear friend, I am praying that all is well with you and that your body is as healthy as I know your soul is.* }

3 JOHN 2 NLT

Seeing her child suffer is the deepest pain a mother can endure. In 1 Kings 17:17-24, we read about a mother who felt the worst possible pain—her son's death. In her excruciation, she bitterly asks the prophet Elijah, whom she has been housing, "What do you have against me, man of God? Did you come to remind me of my sin and kill my son?"

Elijah's response and the subsequent events reveal the heart of God not only for this woman and her child but also for us and our children:

> "Give me your son," Elijah replied. He took him from her arms, carried him to the upper room...and cried to the Lord, "O Lord my God, let this boy's life return to him!"

On behalf of this heartbroken woman, Elijah cried to the Lord for God's healing power to revive her son. Elijah's heart was pained, just as hers was, and God responded to his cry:

> The Lord heard Elijah's cry, and the boy's life returned to him, and he lived.

Malachi speaks of the One whom God would send who, like Elijah, would bear us up in His arms and intercede for our healing:

> But for you who revere my name, the sun of right-
> eousness will rise with healing in its wings.

> MALACHI 4:2

Isaiah also prophesies of God making healing available to us:

> But he was pierced for our transgressions, he was
> crushed for our iniquities; the punishment that brought us
> peace was upon him, and by his wounds we are healed.

> ISAIAH 53:5

Who is the sun of righteousness with healing in His wings? Who is the One who was pierced and crushed, whose wounds have purchased our healing? First Timothy 2:5 identifies Him: "For there is one God and one mediator between God and men, the man Christ Jesus." Jesus is the One who, like Elijah, bears us up in His arms to the place of healing—His Father's presence.

In order to attain the healing Jesus offers, we need two things: His Word and faith. Psalm 107:20 speaks of the former: "He sent forth his word and healed them; he rescued them from the grave." Luke 8:48 speaks of the latter: "Then [Jesus] said to her, 'Daughter, your faith has healed you. Go in peace'" (Luke 8:48).

Jesus has brought us healing, and the way we receive it is by receiving Him through His Word—because He and His Word are one. (See John 1:1-18.) We receive Him with our faith, which comes by hearing the Word of God. (Rom. 8:17.) The most important thing we can do to attain divine healing is to spend time reading, meditating on, speaking, and listening to His Word.

If your children need healing, focus on Scriptures that refer to God's healing nature. In the Old Testament, God told His people, "I am the Lord, who heals you" (Ex. 15:26). Psalm 103:3 says that He "forgives all your sins and heals all your diseases." God is a healer, and He wants you and your kids to be healthy every day of your lives. Mark 6:56 says, "...all who touched [Jesus] were healed." And 3 John 2 says, "Dear friend, I pray that you may enjoy good health and that all may go well with you, even as your soul is getting along well."

You can never overdose on the Word of God, and it works as a preventive medicine as well as a cure. Teach your children to take a regular dose of healing by daily reading and speaking God's Word. Then, if sickness tries to touch anyone in your house, treat it on the spot with the Word of God. God's Word is powerful because it contains His unconquerable will—and His will is your health. Receive and believe His Word, and expect God's healing for your family today.

LIVE ON PURPOSE TODAY

Teach your children this paraphrase of 1 Peter 2:24: "By Jesus' stripes I was healed."

PRAYER

*Father, in Jesus' name, I receive Your healing today. I commit
to study and to instruct my family in Your Word so Your promises
become our daily experience. We receive Your healing touch
in our lives today and every day, in Jesus' name. Amen.*

Your Spiritual Thermostat

*For the kingdom of God is not a matter of eating and drinking,
but of righteousness, peace and joy in the Holy Spirit.*

ROMANS 14:17

Just as we set the thermostat to determine the temperature of our homes, we can set our spiritual thermostats to determine the spiritual atmosphere of our homes. As moms, we have an acute ability to dictate the atmosphere of our homes. When we are full of peace, our children reflect that peace. When we are full of stress, our children reflect that stress. Whatever attitude we demonstrate to our children multiplies in strength through our families and determines the atmospheric pressure of our homes. If we demonstrate peace, peace reigns; if anger, anger storms; and so it goes with any attitude we set on our spiritual thermostats.

The highest standard for our homes' spiritual atmosphere is that of heaven, and Romans 14:17 tells us what that atmosphere is composed of: "righteousness, peace and joy in the Holy Spirit" (Rom. 14:17). When we stay close to heaven by staying close to Jesus, we bring heaven's atmosphere into our homes.

We can't attain by our own effort heaven's righteousness, peace, and joy. They are God's gifts available through a vibrant relationship with Him. When we spend time with Him, and when we draw our family into His presence, we get to experience heaven on earth.

When we live in God's presence, we live in His righteousness. What we do pleases Him because His Word determines our actions and our behavior. The Bible tells us that "Christ Jesus...has become for us wisdom from God–that is, our righteousness, holiness and redemption" (1 Cor. 1:30). We experience heaven's righteousness when Jesus reigns in us, and that happens when we decrease so that He can increase in us. (John 3:30.)

When we live in God's presence, His peace becomes our peace. Jesus said, "Peace I leave with you; my peace I give you. I do not give to you as the world gives. Do not let your hearts be troubled and do not be afraid" (John 14:27). The peace of the world and the peace of Jesus are quite different from one another. While the peace of the world is dependent on circumstances, the peace of Jesus prevails independent of the circumstances. When our families seek God, His peace causes us to remain stable and whole no matter what troubles face us.

When we live in God's presence, we live in His joy. God's joy is impervious to attack. When difficulties arise, God's Word says, "Don't be dejected and sad, for the joy of the Lord is your strength!" (Neh. 8:10). God's joy keeps our families laughing together no matter what happens and attracts our neighbors and friends to Him.

LIVE ON PURPOSE TODAY

Let righteousness, peace, and joy rule in your home today by spending time in God's presence.

But thanks be to God, who always leads us in
triumphal procession in Christ and through us spreads
everywhere the fragrance of the knowledge of him

2 CORINTHIANS 2:14

By welcoming the presence of God into our lives, we
welcome the presence of heaven into our homes. We welcome the
heavenly atmosphere of righteousness, peace, and joy in the Holy
Spirit. When we remain in God, our families find wholeness and
the lost find Him through the fragrance of heaven on us and in
our homes.

PRAYER

Father, I want the atmosphere of Your home to pervade my home.
I will lead my family into Your presence every day so that Your
presence of righteousness, peace, and joy fills us and our home.
Let us consciously carry Your presence with us everywhere we go,
and let Your sweet fragrance on our lives draw many
to You, in Jesus' name. Amen.

Understanding Love

BY SHEILA SMALL

*Greater love hath no man than this, that a man
lay down his life for his friends.*

JOHN 15:13 KJV

I was headed to Professor Conrad's English class with less
than excitement. As usual, he would drone his way through
the lecture with little or no emotion. His iron gray hair, blue
eyes and craggy face only emphasized the boring way he expressed
himself. During class a student asked a question that allowed
Professor Conrad to talk about love. "When you really love
someone you give everything," he said. "There's no 50% or 75%
in love. You give 100%. There's no measurement in the giving or
receiving in unconditional love." Then he started to talk about his
wife and how much he loved her. His eyes twinkled and his voice
was tender. It was not only what he was saying but how that
changed my heart that day. Instantly I saw Professor Conrad in a
new light.

God spoke to me about love through this most unusual
source, and suddenly my heart was changed forever. I had read
about love in 1 Corinthians 13, but after hearing those words, I
began to understand what love really was. Through years of
marriage, children, and grandchildren, as I changed a diaper,
tucked a little one in bed, or prepared a meal when I was almost
too weary to stand, the words "unconditional love" echoed in my

heart and a smile began to weave across my face.

LIVE ON PURPOSE TODAY

First Corinthians 13 says that even the greatest achievements are nothing without love. Check your motivations. If you are lacking in the area of love, then ask God to help you develop this most important gift.

PRAYER

Father God, I want to know Your love better. I want to walk in that love on a regular basis. Teach me more about it. Show me how to act in love. Help me to love others, in Jesus' name. Amen.

Neighboring

BY ANN PLATZ

*They helped every one his neighbor; and every one said
to his brother, Be of good courage.*

ISAIAH 41:6 KJV

Have you ever suspected that the Lord planted you in the very house and neighborhood in which you reside? Oh, you may have thought it was all your own idea. You may have inherited the family estate or settled in this particular neighborhood for economic reasons or with safety precautions in mind. But in the vocabulary of the Christian woman, there is no such thing as *coincidence*.

You may be living here because you are the lone "light" on your street or in your community.

In my design business, I deal with lighting—both interior and exterior. Some houses are "day houses," while others are "night houses." Rooms with large expanses of glass and marvelous exterior views qualify as "day houses." At night, these large glassed-in areas become black "holes," and artificial lighting is needed to soften the darkness.

The houses I call "night houses" are those with strong color and art. These rooms take on a new life at night when lighted properly. Art is enhanced by portrait lights, and directional beams carry the eye to points of interest throughout the house.

Light dispels darkness. Light offers security and protection. Think how welcome you feel when you arrive late at night to find that a lamp has been left on and is still glowing in the window. This message says, "Come in! I care for you. I'm so glad you're home."

For those who live in the home and for neighbors alike, the mature Christian woman is a light, softening the darkness with a message of God's love. Like Florence Nightingale, who lifted her lamp to tend to the wounded soldiers of the Crimean War, she carries God's love with her everywhere she goes. She is the nightlight that offers reassurance. She is the lamp left burning in the window. She is the directional beam, pointing others to the Source of her power.

LIVE ON PURPOSE TODAY

Turn on the light of God's love today, and make a conscious decision to keep the light on.

Ever since Eve, when humankind rejected God's design for intimate fellowship with the Creator, the Lord has waited patiently for each soul to forsake selfishness and look again to Him alone. Weary travelers are looking for a way station, a place to be loved and accepted, a light in the window that says, "We're home." Heart-hungry people need to know that "supper is ready." This is our Lord's call to every human heart: *"I love you. I forgive you. Come to the table, for the feast is prepared."*

As they see Christ in you, operating in love and mercy for your family and others, people in your neighborhood will be attracted to your home. They will feel intuitively that compassion will always be available here, that even a stranger could find refuge.

Cooking a lovely meal to welcome newcomers to the neighborhood, taking a cup of coffee or a tall glass of iced tea to the repairman, or arranging flowers for a neighbor returning home from the hospital are all ways of offering refuge to someone who may be caught in one of life's storms.

We can use our porches and decks, our gardens, our living spaces, our bedrooms, and our eating places as potential harbors. But leave the Light on so that your neighbors can find their way through the darkness.[12]

PRAYER

Father, forgive me for the times when I haven't left the light on—when I haven't seen the needs of others, or when I've forgotten that Your ability inside of me could fill those needs. Holy Spirit, awaken my senses to the needs around me. Help me to constantly shine Your welcoming Light for all to see and be drawn to You. In Jesus' name, I pray. Amen.

Nurturing Your Child's Gift

Your eyes saw my unformed body. All the days
ordained for me were written in your book
before one of them came to be.

PSALM 139:16

E ven before your children were conceived, God had a specific purpose for each one. He knew where and when and to whom they would be born. He knew you would be their mom, and He knew how your training would impact their pursuit of His call.

As a mom, you play a vital role in confirming the purpose of God in each of your children, which He established long before you knew them.

> "I knew you before I formed you in your mother's womb. Before you were born I set you apart and appointed you as my spokesman to the world."
>
> JEREMIAH 1:5 NLT

Your children need to know that they have a unique, God-given purpose—that they were not arbitrarily placed here on earth. They need to know that they are valuable—and their greatest sense of value will come when they know God's value for them, demonstrated in His sacrifice for each one:

For God so loved the world that he gave his only Son,
so that everyone who believes in him will not perish but
have eternal life.

JOHN 3:16 NLT

As your children grow, they will exhibit unique strengths, abilities, and talents. These are gifts from God for their use as they pursue His calling. As a mom, you can help your children discover and develop these unique gifts.

To do this, you will need to spend quality time with your children. As you and your children interact, or simply as all of you go about your day, consciously observe your children's interests and favorite activities. Be aware of their achievements, and be consistent in applauding their efforts.

Most people are sensitive to applause or criticism of their gifts. Keep this in mind as you interact with your children. Your attention and praise will prompt them to continue to use their gifts, but your criticism or disinterest may halt their growth in the area of their giftedness.

In the church God has given us many gifts, and each one has a purpose. It is not to lie dormant but to be used:

LIVE ON PURPOSE TODAY

Talk to your children
about God's gifts in
each of them.

Each one should use whatever gift he has received to serve others, faithfully administering God's grace in its various forms.

1 PETER 4:10

The gift God has given each of us is a demonstration of His grace to be given to others. Encourage your children's efforts to use their gifts to bless others. If your child has the gift of showing mercy, for example, support her as she shows mercy to family members, neighbors, friends, and ministries. If your child is musically talented, encourage him as he uses his gift to worship God and to minister to others. If your child is multital-ented, encourage her to focus on one gift at a time to use to bless others; in time, she will be able to bless others with all of the gifts God has given her.

Sometimes we don't realize the gifts that are within ourselves, let alone within our children. Sometimes it takes more than our physical senses to discern these precious qualities God has placed inside. For this reason, we need to depend on the Holy Spirit as we nurture our children's gifts. He knows God's purpose for each one, and He will enlighten us to see the gifts He has given them to use for His glory.

PRAYER

Father, in Jesus' name, show me the gifts You have placed in my children. Help me to encourage their gifts and their desire to demonstrate Your grace to others by using those gifts. Lord, in Jesus' name, I pray in faith that with their gifts, my children will fulfill Your purpose for Your glory and draw many to You. Amen.

Make Disciples

Therefore go and make disciples of all nations,
baptizing them in the name of the Father and of the
Son and of the Holy Spirit, and teaching them to
obey everything I have commanded you....

MATTHEW 28:19,20

Before His ascension into heaven, Jesus gave His disciples the Great Commission: "Therefore go and make disciples of all nations, baptizing them in the name of the Father and of the Son and of the Holy Spirit, and teaching them to obey everything I have commanded you" (Matt. 28:19,20). His disciples began immediately to spread the word of the glorious gospel of Christ, impacting nations of people. As time passed, the gospel story continued to be told until it reached you, perhaps in a nation far from its Middle Eastern setting. That is because over the past 2000-plus years people have taken to heart Jesus' Great Commission and have made for Him disciples of their acquaintances, friends, parents, siblings, and children.

What has empowered them to carry out the assignment? Has it been human force or willpower? No, it has been the presence of the One who gave the commission, for He said, "And surely I am with you always, to the very end of the age" (Matt. 28:20). In the Person of the Holy Spirit, Christ came to dwell permanently in the earth—in us. In Acts 1:8, Jesus tells His disciples, "But you will receive power when the Holy Spirit comes on you; and you will be my witnesses in Jerusalem, and in all Judea and Samaria, and to the ends of the earth." It is Christ in us who empowers us to make disciples of the nations; it is Christ in you who will empower you to make disciples of your children.

As His disciples today, we too are to carry out this assignment everywhere we go. We have the power—the influence—to be witnesses and make disciples. The family is a great source of interpersonal influence, and God has long used this structure to perpetuate His covenant with His people. For example, in Deuteronomy 11, He speaks directly to parents:

LIVE ON PURPOSE TODAY

Choose a portion of Scripture to study, and look for opportunities to teach your children what you have learned.

Fix these words of mine in your hearts and minds.... Teach them to your children, talking about them when you sit at home and when you walk along the road, when you lie down and when you get up. Write them on the doorframes of your houses and on your gates, so that your days and the days of your children may be many in the land that the Lord swore to give your forefathers, as many as the days that the heavens are above the earth.

DEUTERONOMY 11:18-21

With our words and actions, at every opportunity every day, we are to teach our children the words of God. When we're in the car with them, when we're eating dinner together, we are to speak and live out the words of God. We are to make our children disciples of Christ, as we are disciples of Christ.

In Isaiah 54:13, God promises His people, "All your children shall be taught by the Lord, and great shall be the peace of your children." Claim this verse for your family. It is God's promise, so keep your spiritual ears tuned to His instruction, be ever ready to deliver His instruction to your children, and expect that God Himself will instruct them. Then great will be the peace of your children because they will be disciples of the Prince of Peace.

PRAYER

Father, with joy I accept Your commission to go into the world and make disciples of all nations, baptizing them in the name of the Father and of the Son and of the Holy Spirit, and teaching them to obey everything You have commanded. I desire to make disciples of my children, teaching them Your Word. Thank You for being with me every day, showing me how to teach them personally what You have taught in the Word. Help us as a family to continue to spread the good news of Your love, in Jesus' name. Amen.

When Kids Rebel

*"But while he was still a long way off, his father
saw him and was filled with compassion for him; he ran
to his son, threw his arms around him and kissed him."*

LUKE 15:20

When kids rebel it's tempting to place the blame on someone, and too often mothers blame themselves. The truth is that kids have wills, and they sometimes use them to do the wrong thing—just as all of us have done:

All have sinned and fall short of the glory of God.

ROMANS 3:23

For the first years of our children's lives, we can and should supervise their behavior and attitudes closely. When they rebel against authority, we should lovingly correct them and steer them back onto God's path—which begins with their obedience to us. However, even when children have walked the right path for years, they sometimes stray.

Our longing for our children's well-being is the same longing that our Father feels for each of us. His heart ached when Adam and Eve turned against Him in rebellion, and His heart still aches when any one of us is far from Him. The will God gave each of us gives us the freedom to refuse Him, but we can only imagine the immense joy He feels when we use that will to choose Him!

If your child has chosen to refuse God, you can trust that His Word will light his way back home. (Ps. 119:105.) If your child has wandered from you in rebellion, God wants you to know you are not alone. He has said, "Never will I leave you; never will I forsake you" (Heb. 13:5). He is right by your side, and He won't ever let you or your child go. His eyes are on you and on everything that concerns you—including your child.

If you feel all hope for your child is gone, He gives you this promise: "'There is hope for your future,' says the Lord. 'Your children will come again to their own land'" (Jer. 31:16 NLT). Hold on to God's powerful promise, and speak it over your child every day.

If your heart aches for your child but you don't know what to do, God gives you His Spirit: "Meanwhile, the moment we get tired in the waiting, God's Spirit is right alongside helping us along. If we don't know how or what to pray, it doesn't matter. He does our praying in and for us, making prayer out of our wordless sighs, our aching groans" (Rom. 8:26 MESSAGE). Ask the Holy Spirit to help you pray, and He will help you pray God's will for your child.

The same Intercessor who will lead you in prayer will remind your children of the truth of God's Word. Jesus promised He would:

LIVE ON PURPOSE TODAY

Speak to each of your children about God's love and forgiveness, and reassure them of your unconditional love.

But the Comforter (Counselor, Helper, Intercessor, Advocate, Strengthener, Standby), the Holy Spirit...will teach you all things. And He will cause you to recall (will remind you of, bring to your remembrance) everything I have told you.

JOHN 14:26 AMP

Your children may need a reminder in their hearts of the love and forgiveness that awaits them in God's presence and at home. Even if you can't remind them, the Holy Spirit will—when you pray.

If distance or silence separates you from your child, don't give up on God's ability to bring him back. Entrust your prodigal child to His keeping, and get ready for a joyful reunion—because one day you will see him on the horizon making his way back home.

PRAYER

Father, I entrust my kids to Your care. I commit to loving them unconditionally, praying for them, correcting them, and telling them of Your unconditional love and forgiveness, which You've made available to us through Your Son, Jesus. Holy Spirit, let Your words be my words, and Your attitude be mine as I communicate with my children. I thank You, Lord, that Your peace reigns in my family and that each of us walks in Your light and on Your path, in Jesus' name. Amen.

God Knows

BY TRACIE HUNSBERGER

Remember the former things, those of long ago;
I am God, and there is no other; I am God, and there is
none like me. I make known the end from the beginning,
from ancient times, what is still to come. I say:
My purpose will stand, and I will do all that I please.

ISAIAH 46:9,10 NIV

Two years after I decided not to go to Bible school because of finances, God reminded me that I had made a commitment to Him. I had told Him I would go back to school when my family was out of debt. Really I had made that promise never expecting to get out of debt, yet there I was $15,000 dollars paid off. I never understood why I needed to go back to school; I had been out of school for almost ten years. But I knew I wanted to please God. He said, *Go,* so I went.

The morning of graduation God showed me why it was so important that I had listened to His voice.

Alyssa, my six-year-old daughter, woke up with severe cramps. We rushed her to the emergency room on the morning of graduation. I never dreamed that five days later we would still be there. The tests showed an extra tube on her kidney which was causing a severe infection. The doctors advised surgery immediately and antibiotics for the rest of her life. But God had already

LIVE ON PURPOSE TODAY

You may not understand exactly why God leads you to do certain things, but when you know its God, follow His direction. He always has your best interests in mind.

prepared me. I had learned enough about God to know that He takes care of His kids. I had learned enough about the Bible in school and seen enough in my own life to know about God's faithfulness. He is always there! He is always waiting for us to come to Him so He can help. I prayed and I knew He would show Himself faithful as He always had. Alyssa never had to have surgery; they ran the tests again and were unable to find any reason why Alyssa got so sick. I learned a valuable lesson through all of that. Before God had ever spoken to me He saw what we would go through. He knew how we needed to be prepared. And He sent the provision in advance.

PRAYER

Father God, forgive me if I have not followed Your leading like I should. Help me to get back on track with Your will for my life. Thank You for Your provision in every area, in Jesus' name. Amen.

One Body

In Christ we who are many form one body,
and each member belongs to all the others.

ROMANS 12:5

The word "church" is used to describe both a local body of believers and the corporate body of Christ—believers worldwide for all time. On an eternal scale, it is most important to be a part of the corporate church—and that happens when we believe the Good News and receive salvation. However, without the local church we cannot fully experience, understand, benefit from, or bless the corporate church—the body of Christ.

The local church is an expression of the body of Christ. It is where members of the body spend time together, edify one another, pray with one another, and worship together. It is also where we experience Christ's anointing to a greater degree, enabling us to go out and be witnesses of Him and bring more members in—thus fulfilling His great commission. As Christ's body, we carry His anointing with us individually and corporately. However, until the body begins working together we will never see the fullness of God's anointing.

This work together begins with the meeting of believers— members of the body—together. The local church is where this most often happens. As members of the body of Christ, we need the strength and anointing available from joining with the rest of the members. We need to make time in our schedules to be in church with our families.

As we make the choice to bring our families to church, we need to remember that our children observe not only our choices but our attitudes. They will benefit less if we choose church attendance because we have to, than if we do so because we want to. Remember, David said, "It made me glad to hear them say, 'Let's go to the house of the Lord!'" (Ps. 122:1). Imagine how your attitude can affect your children if you say with a genuine smile on your face, "Let's go to church!" That smile will come when time in church equates to time in God's presence, being built up in His Word, and joining with the rest of His body to worship Him.

It is no coincidence that the Holy Spirit came to rest on individuals when they were all together worshiping Him on the day of Pentecost. After Jesus' resurrection, He told His followers, "Do not leave Jerusalem, but wait for the gift my Father promised, which you have heard me speak about. For John baptized with water, but in a few days you will be baptized with the Holy Spirit" (Acts 1:4). As the believers unified in obedience, reverence, faith, and trust, they received the promise. As a result, they became witnesses to Jerusalem and to the ends of the earth. Christ and His anointing became manifested in the earth through individuals as they joined in worshipping Him.

LIVE ON PURPOSE TODAY

Make an appointment to join with other members of Christ's body to worship and to serve Him together.

Imagine what God can do in and through His body when we continue to unify, joining in one place at one time to honor the one God. This week, make your choice. And remember: Your children are watching.

PRAYER

Father, in Jesus' name, I thank You for making me a member of the body of Christ. Help me and my family to unite with other members of the body to worship You and to fulfill Your work. Show us our place in the body so that we can serve You well by serving others. Amen.

God's Ideals

*But he said to me, "My grace is sufficient for you,
for my power is made perfect in weakness."
Therefore I will boast all the more gladly about my
weaknesses, so that Christ's power may rest on me.*

2 CORINTHIANS 12:9

Whatever ideals we have in life, we hold one close to our hearts: We each want to be the perfect mom for our kids. Though every mom's definition of *the perfect mom* is slightly different from the next, every mom has one thing in common: imperfection. The problem is that we're all human, and that means we all fall short of ideal. (Rom. 3:23.)

Ask any mom in the world if she's ever had a moment when she didn't like being a mom, and if she's honest she'll say yes. It's not that she's ever stopped loving her kids, but she has had moments—or even days—when she didn't like the job of mother-hood. Those are the days when she feels less than ideal.

The truth is that God isn't into human idealism. He thinks, sees, and feels on a completely different level than we do. He says to each of us,

> For as the heavens are higher than the earth, so are
> my ways higher than your ways, and my thoughts than
> your thoughts.

ISAIAH 55:9

God wants us to let go of our human ideals and standards and cling to Him. He wants us to focus on His strength and His ability to follow His commands—not our own weakness and inability to accomplish our own.

When we demand more of ourselves than God does, we limit our progress in Him. As moms, that means we limit our progress in relationship to our children. God wants each of us to become so dependent on the leading of His Word and His Spirit that we set aside our own agendas and our own ideals and follow solely after His. He wants us to rise above our perspective so that we achieve His.

Until we see our lives as He does, we won't realize the differences between our ideals and His. For example, what we see as a failure, God may see as a victory. We may see a messy kitchen as a failure, but God may see the victory we won by spending extra time attending to our children's needs. We may see an angry outburst as a failure, but God may see the progress we made by responding to a wrongdoing with justice.

LIVE ON PURPOSE TODAY

Seek God to discover His agenda for your day, and follow it in His strength.

Until we gain God's perspective on our lives, we may be chasing after an ideal, pressing ourselves to a mark that God never intended us to reach. If we run after our ideals rather than His, we will miss His mark—the only one that matters. But if we press toward His, we will reach it—but not by our own efforts. What we need now, and what we will always need, is God's grace—and in our weakness, He has offered us a sufficient supply. (2 Cor. 12:9.) When we depend on the leading of His Word and His Spirit, and when we settle into the gift of His grace, we become who God wants us to be. May this become our ideal.

PRAYER

Father, thank You for Your grace which You freely gave me through the gift of Your Son, Jesus. I ask You to forgive me for chasing after my own ideals rather than Yours. Teach me how to be the mom You want me to be—to place value on what You value and to walk in Your anointing in relationship to my kids. Father, I release my own agenda and commit to press toward Yours in Your strength. Thank You, Lord, that Your mercies are new every morning and Your grace is sufficient for me, in Jesus' name. Amen.

Children, Honor Your Parents

Honor your father and your mother, as the
Lord your God has commanded you, so that
you may live long and that it may go well with
you in the land the Lord your God is giving you.

DEUTERONOMY 5:16

The greatest reward we can have as mothers is to know that our children honor God on a personal level—not just at home, but everywhere they go; not just when they're living with us, but when they've moved out and established their own adult lives. To receive this reward, we teach them at home how to honor God in everything they say and do.

God has a plan and a destination for each of our children. He knows the gifts He wants them to use, the people He wants to minister to through them, and the blessings He wants to give them. However, He gives them a clear command to follow in order to reach and enjoy the place to which He has called them: They must honor their parents.

Though our children are ultimately accountable for honoring or dishonoring us, we can help them make the right choice. To do that, we will need to keep in mind the position in which God has placed us in our homes. Only then will our children understand and respect authority.

The Bible often addresses children, specifically directing them to obey their parents. (Eph. 6:1; Col. 3:20.) If God says that our children must obey us, that means we must do something as well. First Timothy 3:4 says, "He must manage his own family well and see that his children obey him with proper respect." If we don't require our children to obey and respect us, we give them room to disobey and disrespect not only our authority but every human's authority and, ultimately, God's.

Our children's first step toward learning to honor God is honoring us. Responsibility and honor begin at home under parental instruction, and continue throughout life. As parents, we give our children every opportunity to succeed in life when we require them to follow the commandment to honor us.

When we make this requirement, we must be sure that we base our authority on the Word of God. We must lead as He leads. We must honor our word—doing what we say we will do. We must show grace, caring more about each child's well-being than our own agenda. We must reward diligence. We must be motivated by love. In short, we must learn who our Father is and reflect Him to our children.

When we teach our children to honor us and to honor God, we give them the precious opportunity to avoid all of the pain and frustration that rebellion and disrespect ultimately bring, and we

LIVE ON PURPOSE TODAY

Do your children honor and obey you? If not, make a plan today to help them learn how.

lead them to the land the Lord their God is giving them. That is what true love can do, and that is what we do when we honor God's Word by teaching our children to honor Him.

PRAYER

Father, I want my children to honor You all of their days.
Help me daily to realize my responsibility in teaching them to
honor You. Help me to base my expectations of them on Your Word
and to be led by Your Holy Spirit as I train them in Your way.
Thank You for the plans You have for each one of them—plans to
prosper them in the places to which You've called them. Use me to
help them choose Your path, Lord. In Jesus' name I pray. Amen.

Spiritual Warfare

BY ANN PLATZ

Be careful! Watch out for attacks from the Devil,
your great enemy. He prowls around like a
roaring lion, looking for some victim to devour.
Take a firm stand against him, and be strong in your faith.

1 PETER 5:8,9 NLT

When we are involved in kingdom work, we are fair game for harassment and attack in the spiritual realm. Before I began my deeper walk with God, I was completely ignorant of the fact that we, as Christians, are engaged in a war. I was enjoying a stroll in the park while more seasoned warriors were doing hand-to-hand combat with the enemy of our souls—Satan.

"Onward, Christian Soldiers" was merely an old hymn, one that is sung seldom, if ever, anymore. But I was uninitiated in such matters. For one thing, I hadn't the faintest notion of what soldiers do—other than the fact that they look wonderful in their uniforms, march in parades, and fight in wartime. Well-bred Southern ladies are taught, from birth, to look for the positive aspects of any situation, to maintain one's composure, and to be polite in any event. Hardly the substance of soldiering.

When I discovered that I must regroup and retrain, I asked my husband to tell me something about war. As John talked, I took notes, scribbling frantically:

"War is a science," he began. "First of all, an army never goes into battle without being fully informed about the enemy they will engage. What is the nature of the enemy? What kinds of tactics are likely to be used? What kinds of battle strategies have been employed in past confrontations?

"Next, an army must be armed and prepared—both offensively and defensively. Keeping in mind the possible strategies that may be used, training begins and weapons are issued.

"Plans call for strikes and counteroffensives to be devised and coordinated. In training, soldiers are drilled until they can react instantaneously and without forethought.

"An army cannot function without provisions. Food, fuel, and ammunition must be carried to the battlefield, and extra supplies and reinforcements ready for delivery."

John paused, looking off into space as he thought. "But above all," he concluded, "an army doesn't go into battle without being determined to win."

Immediately I could see parallels for spiritual warfare. I learned more about the face of our enemy as I searched the Scriptures for everything I could find on Satan, Lucifer, the father of lies, the "prince of darkness."

He is devious and cunning. He is out to rob, kill, and destroy. He is often disguised as an angel of light. It gets worse:

We are not fighting against people made of flesh and blood, but against persons without bodies—the evil rulers of the unseen world, those mighty satanic beings and great evil princes of darkness who rule this world; and against huge numbers of wicked spirits in the spirit world.

EPHESIANS 6:12 TLB

But the more I read, the more excited I became. God has not left us without a plan, advice about preparation for battle, and provisions—"the full armor of God"—that is able to help us overtake and defeat our enemy.

LIVE ON PURPOSE TODAY

Put on each piece of spiritual armor God has provided for you, and go to battle confident of victory.

Use every piece of God's armor to resist the enemy whenever he attacks, and when it is all over, you will still be standing up. But to do this, you will need the strong belt of truth and the breastplate of God's approval. Wear shoes that are able to speed you on as you preach the Good News of peace with God. In every battle you will need faith as your shield to stop the fiery arrows aimed at you by Satan. And you will need the helmet of salvation and the sword of the Spirit—which is the Word of God.

Pray all the time. Ask God for anything in line with the Holy Spirit's wishes. Plead with him, reminding him of your needs, and keep praying earnestly for all Christians everywhere.

EPHESIANS 6:13-18 TLB

Be on guard. Sometimes the enemy launches surprise attacks. The strongest ones may come from within the family. When you are aware of the enemy's strategies, you can see the plan for division—mother against daughter, father against son. It is sad when families are separated; it may take generations to restore fellowship.

Every day, as we prepare to face the next twenty-four-hour period with its inevitable skirmishes with the enemy, we must put on the whole armor of God, not leaving out one single item that is designed for our safety and protection. Then we can step out into our world, eyes fixed on our Commander, confident of victory![13]

PRAYER

Father, I am alert in prayer. I am aware of the enemy who seeks to kill, steal, and destroy. Therefore, I put on my spiritual armor—the belt of truth, the breastplate of righteousness, the marching boots of peace, the shield of faith, the helmet of salvation, the sword of the Spirit—the Word of God. I pray in the Spirit with perseverance for all the saints, who stand beside me in this battle, looking unto You, our victorious Commander. Lead us to battle, Lord. We will follow You to victory, in Jesus' name. Amen.

Mothering Your Adult Children

God desires that our children learn through our training how to meet the responsibilities that will face them as adults. Once they get there, He desires that we let them meet the challenges of adulthood in His strength. After years of training, they may be more ready for the transition than we are!

For example, when our adult children are faced with important decisions, we may wish we could decide for them. However, we need to consider what God's Word says: "Train up a child in the way he should go, and when he is old he will not depart from it" (Prov. 22:6 NKJV). If we have trained them in the way they should go, we can trust that they will discern God's will for their own lives.

If we haven't trained them in God's ways, their adulthood is not the time for us to start. We need to ask God to father them, Jesus to befriend them, and the Holy Spirit to lead them—and we need to be prepared to offer godly instruction when our children ask. In the meantime, our best ministry tools for reaching them will be our prayers and our godly and loving example.

Even if we think our well-trained children are making unwise decisions, we need to be careful how we respond. If their hearts are open to God's voice, they will know His will for their lives—even more than we will. At this point in their lives, we can help them most by praying for them, encouraging them, and reinforcing our belief in them.

No matter how mature our children become, they will always benefit from knowing we believe in them. Their desire to delight us doesn't stop in preschool, when they beam at their colored pictures on the refrigerator door. That desire for our approval lasts for a lifetime. Knowing their parents are proud of them will give our adult children the assurance they need to confidently reach for their God-given dreams.

If we ourselves haven't received this kind of affirmation from our parents, it may feel uncomfortable to give it to our kids. However, if we want our children to live satisfied and fulfilled lives, we will make the extra effort to demonstrate our love, belief, and delight in them. Remember: Before Jesus entered His earthly ministry, His Father affirmed Him, saying, "You are My beloved Son, in whom I am well pleased" (Mark 1:11).

We should never stop telling our children how pleased we are with

LIVE ON PURPOSE TODAY

With a note or a phone call, tell each of your kids, "I love you, I believe in you, and I am proud of you."

them, how beloved they are in our eyes, and how much joy it gives us to call them our own. When we love them like this, we give them the courage to be the men and women God created them to be—and we give ourselves the gift of a fulfilling and lasting relationship with each one of them.

PRAYER

Father, in Jesus' name, I pray that You would speak clearly to my children today. Give them wisdom to face every challenge, and provide for every one of their needs. I ask You to give Your angels charge over my children to protect them. Holy Spirit, convict my children when they head the wrong way, and lead them on God's blessed path for their lives. Help me to be an affirming mom who freely loves my children with the love You have given me. Amen.

Instructions for Marriage

For the husband is the head of the wife as Christ is the head of the church, his body, of which he is the Savior. Now as the church submits to Christ, so also wives should submit to their husbands in everything. Husbands, love your wives, just as Christ loved the church.... Each one of you also must love his wife as he loves himself, and the wife must respect her husband.

EPHESIANS 5:23-26,33

T
hrough the Bible God has given us instructions for marriage that, if followed, will create joyful and lifelong unions between us and our husbands. He has shown us that in His divine structure for the family, the husband (the head of the home) is to love his wife as Christ (the head of the church) loves the church. (Eph. 5:2,3). He is also to love her as he loves himself. (v. 33.) The wife is to submit to her husband as the church submits to Christ (v. 24), and she is to respect him. (v. 33.)

In Christ, we see a picture of the love God wants to give us through our husbands—an unconditional love that would do anything to ensure our well-being, peace, joy—everything we need to live an abundant life. In self-love, He has given us another example of a blessed relationship between a man and his wife. For a man to love his wife as he loves himself, he must share the highest level of trust, honesty, and respect with her.

In the church, we see a picture of the submission we are to give our husbands. To submit is to have "a voluntary attitude of giving in" to our husbands, "cooperating" with them, "assuming responsibility" with and for them, and "carrying" their "burden[s]."[14] A woman who willfully chooses to submit to—give in to, cooperate with, assume responsibility for, and carry the burdens of—her husband, is a content, happy, and blessed woman.

Submission requires the trust, honesty, and respect that naturally come when a husband loves his wife as Christ loves the church and as he loves himself. True submission from a wife to her husband says, "I respect you and your God-given place of leadership in our home; therefore, I yield to your judgment, trusting that you will lead our family toward God's best for us."

Our marriages depend on our submission to and respect for our husbands as much as they depend on our husbands' love for us. God holds our husbands—the head of the home—ultimately responsible for the condition of our families. We need to recognize and respect their God-given role by cooperating with them, assuming responsibility with them, and carrying their burdens so that our families can continue toward the land of God's best for us. When we allow God's Word to guide our families, that is exactly where He will lead us.

LIVE ON PURPOSE TODAY

Think of five things you can do today to improve your relationship with your husband.

PRAYER

*Father, in Jesus' name, I praise You for the gift of my husband.
I ask You to lead me in my relationship with him so that I can
bless him as the wife You desire for him. Father, I pray that
You'll direct my husband and me in every area of our marriage so
that we increasingly reflect the picture of Christ and the church.
I choose to honor and obey Your Word, Lord. Amen.*

The Help of the Holy Spirit

May the grace of the Lord Jesus Christ, and the love of God, and the fellowship of the Holy Spirit be with you all.

2 CORINTHIANS 13:14 NIV

Today, our kids face all kinds of challenges in this world—peer pressure, rejection, and violence, just to name a few. As mothers today, we need something more than our five senses to keep our kids healthy and whole. We need help! Thank God, He has given us everything we need in the gift of the Holy Spirit, our Helper. Jesus said,

> ...you...know how to give good gifts to your children. But your heavenly Father is even more ready to give the Holy Spirit to anyone who asks.

LUKE 11:13 CEV

When we ask the Father for the gift of the Holy Spirit, He sends Him to dwell in us:

> Do you not know that your body is the temple (the very sanctuary) of the Holy Spirit Who lives within you, Whom you have received [as a Gift] from God? You are not your own.

1 CORINTHIANS 6:19 AMP

When we moms fellowship with the Holy Spirit, we become sensitive to what He sees, hears, and knows about our children. The Bible offers many examples of how the Holy Spirit can help us, and we can apply each to our maternal responsibilities.

Acts 13:4 NIV says that Barabas and Paul were "sent on their way by the Holy Spirit." Just as the Holy Spirit sent Barabas and Paul on their ministry journey, He will help us direct our lives and the lives of our children. As we listen to His voice in our hearts, we will be able to help our children stay on His path for their lives.

As we fellowship with the Holy Spirit, He will also help us discern the integrity of the people around them. Acts 13:9 NIV tells us that Paul, "filled with the Holy Spirit," was able to discern and rebuke a man who was being motivated by the devil. Knowing what motivates a person will help us protect our children from those who would cause them harm.

When we spend time with the Holy Spirit, He will help us teach our children exactly what they need to know, when they need to know it. (See Acts 15:28 NIV.) When we rely on the Holy Spirit to train our children, they will understand and retain the knowledge we share with them.

As we instruct our children, the Holy Spirit will fill our mouths with

LIVE ON PURPOSE TODAY

Listen for the voice of the Holy Spirit regarding each of your children, and follow His instructions.

His words. (See 2 Peter 1:21.) When we listen to the Holy Spirit, we can deliver a message straight from heaven to our children.

Perhaps the greatest benefit of knowing the Holy Spirit is having His help in praying for our kids:

> And the Holy Spirit helps us in our distress. For we don't even know what we should pray for, nor how we should pray. But the Holy Spirit prays for us with groanings that cannot be expressed in words.
>
> ROMANS 8:26 NLT

The Holy Spirit is our comforter, counselor, helper, intercessor, advocate, strengthener, and standby. (John 14:26 AMP.) He is a precious friend to us as mothers, and He wants to help us keep our kids healthy, whole, and prospering. When we give Him our lives, He can accomplish it all through us.

PRAYER

Father, in Jesus' name, I receive the help of the Holy Spirit. Holy Spirit, enlighten me with Your wisdom and insight regarding my children, and pray God's perfect will through me for them, in Jesus' name. Amen.

Kick Out Guilt

G uilt is a motivator. If we allow it to, it can convince us to do some pretty foolish things. Sometimes our actions welcome guilt into our lives, but often it sneaks up on us without our ever realizing that it's completely out of place.

For example, a new mom may feel guilty for making time for herself away from her baby—even just to take a shower. Another mom may feel guilty for not being able to give her child something that "all the other kids have." A working mom may feel guilty for not spending more time with her child. A stay-at-home mom may feel guilty for not helping make money for the family. Whatever the reason, many moms suffer from at least occasional bouts of guilt.

While it seems that guilt can lead us out of error, the opposite is actually often true. Guilt can make us aware of a problem inside, but it can't enable us to change. In fact, it often arrests our progress by blinding us to the solution—which is faith. Hebrews 10:19-22 says:

Therefore, brothers, since we have confidence to enter the Most Holy Place by the blood of Jesus, by a new and living way opened for us through the curtain, that is, his body, and since we have a great priest over the house of God, let us draw near to God with a sincere heart in full assurance of faith, having our hearts sprinkled to cleanse us from a guilty conscience and having our bodies washed with pure water.

Guilt and faith are counteractive motivators. Guilt holds us in our prison of dissatisfaction with self, while faith urges us onward and upward. By faith, we draw near to the One who can cleanse us from guilt.

When we try to appease our guilt by ourselves, we often make mistakes—which lead to more guilt. But when our hearts are sprinkled clean from guilt, we gain God's perspective and make changes in His power.

LIVE ON PURPOSE TODAY

As you go about your day, be motivated by love—never guilt.

Sure, we make mistakes, but the solution is not to wallow in guilt. The solution is Jesus:

So now there is no condemnation for those who belong to Christ Jesus.

ROMANS 8:1 NLT

When you make a mistake and guilt slaps you in the face, don't grab it and hold on to it to punish yourself. Let it go and reach with both hands for the One who can cleanse you and pull you up to the only expectation that truly matters—His own.

PRAYER

Father, in Jesus' name, Your Word says that if we confess our sins, You are faithful and just to forgive us our sins. (1 John 1:9.) Lord, I repent for my sins, and I thank You that You do not condemn me. I put the past behind me, and I ask You to give me Your perspective of me. Help me walk in the victory over guilt that You've already won for me so that my only motivation in life is Your love, in Jesus' name. Amen.

A Grandmother's Love

*I have been reminded of your sincere faith, which first
lived in your grandmother Lois and in your mother
Eunice and, I am persuaded, now lives in you also.*

2 TIMOTHY 1:5

Through the lineage of Abraham, Isaac, Jacob, and all the way to Joseph and finally Jesus, we can see the value God places on family ties. And it's not so much the bloodline that matters: Mary conceived Jesus by the Holy Spirit, not by Joseph. What matters most is relationship.

A grandmother's relationship with God yields eternal fruit. Believing grandmothers have the opportunity to exemplify God's faithfulness and the blessing of a life spent with Him. The apostle Paul speaks of the treasure of such a grandmother in 2 Timothy 1:5: "I have been reminded of your sincere faith, which first lived in your grandmother Lois and in your mother Eunice and, I am persuaded, now lives in you also." What a blessed woman Lois was to impact the second and third generations with her personal faith, and how blessed Timothy was to benefit from her influence!

Through a grandmother, God can hand down great blessing and wisdom to the next generations. Whether she has walked with God her whole life or only recently come to know Him, a grandmother can speak into her children's and grandchildren's lives the priceless wisdom attained through personal experience.

Titus speaks of the influence she can have when she is reverent in the way she lives and teaches what is good. (Titus 2:3.)

In the book of Ruth, we find a woman whose prayers, love, and godly influence impacted innumerable generations to follow. Through her loving influence with her widowed daugher-in-law, Naomi helped a union begin between Ruth and Boaz. As a result of their union, Naomi became the grandmother-in-love to Obed, whom she loved as her very own child. (Ruth 4:16.) Years later, her influence would reach King David, the grandson of Obed. Naomi's prayers and love yielding a worshipful shepherd-turned-king after God's own heart, the Great Shepherd, and ultimately all who would believe in Christ and become God's blood-bought sons and daughters.

As moms and grandmothers, we must never underestimate the profound and eternal impact we make on future generations every day. If we ask Him to, God will equip us with His wisdom to share with our children and grandchildren. Even if we cannot be with them, we can touch them with His love and influence—through our prayers.

LIVE ON PURPOSE TODAY

With a note, a phone call, or a prayer, reach out to your children and grandchildren with a personal touch of God's love today.

PRAYER

Father, I ask You to be with my children and grandchildren. Holy Spirit, draw them close to You. I ask You to protect, guide, deliver, and save each one. I commit to keeping Your commands, Lord, and I pray that my children will, too, "so that it might go well with them and their children forever" (Deut. 5:29). I entrust each one to You, Lord, and I thank You that their lives bless You and every generation to come, in Jesus' name. Amen.

Know Him

*Trust in the Lord with all thine heart; and lean
not unto thine own understanding. In all thy ways
acknowledge him, and he shall direct thy paths.*

PROVERBS 3:5,6 KJV

G od wants you. He doesn't just want your warm body in
the church building or your occasional prayer for a need
or at the dinner table. He wants you.

God wants to be closer to you than your heartbeat, and He
wants you to know He is there with you all the time. That is why
He sent His Holy Spirit—so that you could have His perpetual
presence inside. The Holy Spirit confirms in your heart that God is
your Father. (Rom. 5:5; Eph. 1:13.) He empowers you to do, to
pray, and to speak God's will every day. (Acts 10:38; 1 Peter 1:21.)
He comforts you; He fills you with hope (Rom. 15:13); He teaches
you (Luke 12:12; John 14:26); and He strengthens you with His
joy. (Luke 10:21; Acts 13:52.)

God wants to direct you by His Spirit every day, and the
Bible says that when you acknowledge Him in all your ways you
enable Him to do just that. Acknowledging Him means knowing
Him, perceiving Him, distinguishing Him from others, knowing
Him by experience, recognizing Him, admitting and confessing
that He is there, and considering His presence.[15] Acknowledging
Him in all your ways means acknowledging Him all day, every
day. Whether you're doing the laundry, reading to your kids, or

watching television, He wants you to be consciously aware of His presence.

When we are conscious of God's presence all day, every day, our behavior changes. We not only steer clear of sin, but we walk in step with God's victorious plan every moment. Proverbs 3:6 says that when we acknowledge Him in all our ways, "he shall direct [our] paths." Our acknowledgment of God's presence enables us to hear His direction throughout each day, which will always lead us to His best gifts for us, as Isaiah says:

> Thus says the Lord, your Redeemer, the Holy One of Israel: I am the Lord your God, Who teaches you to profit, Who leads you in the way that you should go.
>
> ISAIAH 48:17 AMP

God wants to teach us to profit in everything we do. He wants to lead us every moment in "the way that [we] should go." That means He wants to teach us how to train our kids, to do our jobs, to love our husbands, to be good friends—to do everything we do—His way.

LIVE ON PURPOSE TODAY

Live aware of God's presence and follow His leading all day today. Make note of the results.

Just think. We have been given access to a personal assistant who will guide us perfectly every moment of every day. With Him, we can't go wrong. We can clean the house more efficiently than ever before; we can train our kids in a way that's custom-fit for each one of them and for us; we can find true rest; we can love others wholly—all with His help. His name is Holy Spirit, and He guarantees our success in life—in truth, He guarantees life itself. (2 Cor. 1:21.)

Give the Lord your life by acknowledging His presence with you every day. He'll give you true life—abundantly.

PRAYER

Father, I want to be Yours. I dedicate myself wholly to You. I lean on, trust in, and am confident in You in all my ways. Thank You that You direct my paths. Holy Spirit, be a part of every moment of my life, and lead me continually in Your ways. Thank You for Your anointing to walk Your path all of my days, in Jesus' name. Amen.

Spiritual Daughters

O God, you have helped me from my earliest childhood....
Now that I am old and gray, don't forsake me.
Give me time to tell this new generation
(and their children too) about all your mighty miracles."

PSALM 71:17,18 TLB

I remember holding my first child, Courtney, in my arms only hours after she was born. I started speaking to her then, and I haven't stopped since. Ours has been such a dear mentoring relationship.

A mother usually has more influence over her daughters than any other woman does. In everything she does, she is preparing her children for adulthood, setting the standards for their future home.

Once when I came home from boarding school as a teenager, I found that my room had been beautifully redecorated. Mother had chosen peach floral wallpaper with ferns and flowers everywhere. It was very pretty—although I didn't particularly like the colors and wouldn't have chosen them for myself. There was nothing at all unacceptable about the room—it just wasn't me. My mother's goal had been to complete her redecorating project when it would least inconvenience my sister and me. It probably never occurred to her to include me in the selection process.

When my own daughters came along, I remembered this and decided to involve them in the decorating decisions for their rooms, even though they were under five at the time. "I like this, Mommy" was music to my ears as we chose fabric and wallpaper.

Think about the things you want to pass on to your daughters. Are they learning the deeper lessons of life, as well as good interior design and lovely manners? Do they know how their grandparents met, your mother's funniest moment, and other family stories?

Will they know how to set up their own households when the time comes? I don't know what I would have done without my mother's expertise. She moved all four of her children into our respective houses, arriving at our doorstep on moving day, equipped with helpers and painters and whatever else was needed. Mother was the commander of a small army on a mission of mercy. It's one of my favorite memories.

By my mother did far more for us than teach us about homemaking. She followed the biblical exhortation to train up her children in the admonition of the Lord. She taught us the commandments and wisdom of God. She modeled hospitality and instructed us to be good citizens, to put on compassion, kindness, humility, gentleness, and patience. We learned how to forgive and to live together in unity.

Sadly, many women have not had the guidance they have needed. Their mothers either couldn't or wouldn't teach, love, and instruct their daughters. So many women are emotionally unavailable to their children.

Some have lost their mothers to death. A close friend whose mother died when she was a teenager sweetly invited me to point out anything that her mother would have taught during those last teenage years, especially in matters of etiquette. Of course I agreed but, to this day, I haven't felt the need to tell her anything. Her request did, however, cause me to ponder the value of a mother's instruction and how much she is missed when she's gone.

These are among the reasons so many women mentors are presently being used mightily by God. When I mentioned Kay Arthur's name to a lady, she quickly responded, "She's my spiritual mother." Kay had never met this dear woman, but through Kay's video lectures and books she has "mothered" others in their Christian faith. She has many, many spiritual children.

One of the most precious aspects of mentoring is the feeling that those under your care become like your children—beloved, encouraged, restored, and sent forth into the world with their vision a little clearer and in focus.

In celebrating life, we truly pass on to the next generation wisdom that could be of great benefit. Maybe we will teach such great lessons and younger women will learn so well that they can avoid the pitfalls we suffered at their age. Many will cherish the opportunity to connect with the older generation. Think what we could all learn from each other. Older women could be inspired by the energy and optimism of the young; younger women could profit from our

LIVE ON PURPOSE TODAY

Open your heart to God's continuing work inside, and allow Him to minister guidance, hope, and love to those around you.

wisdom and learn from our mistakes. It's funny how this works, isn't it? By giving freely, from your heart, of what you have learned, you ensure that the knowledge and truth you have gained are passed on.[16]

PRAYER

Father, thank You so much for the opportunity to share with my children and others around me the lessons I've learned in this lifetime. Help me to be transparent, willingly sharing from my heart so that others can learn from my experiences—both my victories and my shortcomings. Thank You for working in me and through me to give Your hope and light to a new generation, in Jesus' name. Amen.

More

With God, there is no end. There is no limit to what He can do in and through and for you. In His Word, God has given you everything you need in this life on earth and in the life to come. Salvation, healing, provision, peace, completeness, soundness—these words only begin to describe what God wants to give you—and will give you when you seek Him.

God values you so much that He never, ever wants you to stop receiving gifts from Him. You see, He has already given you everything you need—the only thing left for you to do is receive it. When you start to dig into the truth of His Word, you'll discover that it is His endless treasure for you. You'll keep finding more—more wisdom, more encouragement, more joy, more forgiveness, more mercy, more strength—more of everything you could ever desire. And the more you find, the more you'll want. You'll echo the cry of the Psalmist:

> As the deer pants for streams of water, so my soul
> pants for you, O God.
>
> PSALM 42:1

You'll feel a deep hunger inside growing, and the only thing that will fill it is Him, for "He satisfies the thirsty and fills the hungry with good things" (Ps. 107:9). God wants you to seek Him daily—to read His Word, to listen to the voice of His Spirit inside, to simply rest in Him—so He can satisfy your thirst and fill your hunger with good things—with Him.

As you are filled with Him, you will be changed. You will decrease, and He will increase. In your weakness, He will be shown strong. Day by day, as you walk in His Spirit and not according to the flesh, you will become an increasingly clear reflection of God's glory:

> And we, who with unveiled faces all reflect the Lord's glory, are being transformed into his likeness with ever-increasing glory, which comes from the Lord, who is the Spirit.
>
> 2 CORINTHIANS 3:18

God wants to reveal more of Himself to you so that you become more like Him. He wants to increase in you and your children in every area of life so that you become an increasingly clear image of Him. He wants to complete you. In a salutation to the Corinthians, the apostle Paul wrote, "Finally, brethren, rejoice,

LIVE ON PURPOSE TODAY

Expect more of God—
both for you and
for your children.

be made complete..." (2 Cor. 13:11). The entire purpose of His precious Word is to complete you. When you dig into His treasure, you aim for completion in Him.

Today you can know Him and you can become increasingly like Him through His Word, and one day you will see Him face to face:

> Now we see but a poor reflection as in a mirror; then we shall see face to face. Now I know in part; then I shall know fully, even as I am fully known.
>
> 1 CORINTHIANS 13:12

Give Him all you have—and get ready for more.

PRAYER

Father, I want more of You. I love you with all my heart, with all my soul, and with all my strength. My entire being hungers and thirsts for nothing but You. Fill me, transform me, and use me for Your glory. Let me see You more clearly and reflect You more purely each day, in Jesus' name. Amen.

Give Them Everything

"...whoever accepts and trusts the Son gets in
on everything, life complete and forever!"

JOHN 3:36 MESSAGE

As moms, we want to give our kids everything they need. More than anything else in life, our kids need Jesus. Indeed, He is everything they will ever need. His lordship guarantees true, abundant life—beginning on earth and extending into eternity.

In the beginning, before sin entered the world, humanity lived spiritually in communion with God. However, with the entrance of sin came spiritual death and separation from Him. In order to reclaim His beloved creation, God sent Jesus:

> "For God so loved the world that he gave his one and only Son, that whoever believes in him shall not perish but have eternal life."
>
> JOHN 3:16

As the substitute for the sin of humanity, Jesus laid down His life in order to give us His eternal life. At the cross, Jesus saw each of us and each of our children reuniting with the Father. That picture impelled Him to sacrifice everything for us:

> Let us fix our eyes on Jesus, the author and perfecter
> of our faith, who for the joy set before him endured the
> cross, scorning its shame, and sat down at the right hand of
> the throne of God.

HEBREWS 12:2

Now we have the opportunity to receive His gift in our own lives and to share it with our children. We don't have to do anything difficult to receive it. In fact, there is nothing we can do to earn it. The Bible tells us:

> It is by grace you have been saved, through faith—and
> this not from yourselves, it is the gift of God—not by works,
> so that no one can boast.

EPHESIANS 2:8,9

God freely gave us the gift of salvation through His Son, and now the only thing left for us to do is to receive it by believing the message and acknowledging our belief with our words.

LIVE ON PURPOSE TODAY

Share the Gospel message with your children and give them the opportunity to say, "Jesus is my Lord."

The word is near you, in your mouth and in your heart (that is, the word of faith which we preach): that if you confess with your mouth the Lord Jesus and believe in your heart that God has raised Him from the dead, you will be

saved. For with the heart one believes unto righteousness,
and with the mouth confession is made unto salvation.

ROMANS 10:8-10 NKJV

In order to receive this gift from God, we need to hear the
Word—the message of the Cross; we need to confess Jesus as
Lord; and we need to believe in our hearts that God raised Jesus
from the dead.

To share the eternal gift of life with our kids, we simply
need to tell them the Gospel message, then ask them if they
believe and want to confess Jesus as Lord. It's as simple as saying,
"Jesus is my Lord." When they do this, they will be completely
changed spiritually. Second Corinthians 5:17 says, "Therefore, if
anyone is in Christ, he is a new creation; the old has gone, the
new has come!" Their spirits will be reborn, and the Holy Spirit
within them will confirm that God is their Father. (Gal. 4:6.)

Give your children the gift that will change them forever.
Give them everything: Give them Jesus.

PRAYER

*Father, in Jesus' name, I believe the Gospel message—that You
sent Jesus to die for me and that You raised Him from the dead.
I acknowledge Jesus as Lord, and I am a new person. Give me the
words to speak to my children to lead them into a saving knowledge
of You. I will faithfully deliver the Word of faith, and I will
lead them to You as soon as they're ready. Thank You, Lord,
for the abundant life You have given us. Amen.*

Endnotes

1 *Ask Dr. Sears,* "Seven Ways to Bond With Your Preborn Baby," http://www.askdrsears.com/html/1/T010608.asp.

2 Platz, pp. 19-21.

3 Ibid, pp. 43-45.

4 Strong's, #1411.

5 Thayer, s.v. pisidia, Strong's #4098.

6 Platz, pp. 50.51.

7 Ibid, pp. 59-60.

8 Ibid, pp. 87-88.

9 Easton, s.v. "yoke."

10 1 Timothy 5:9 NASB says, "A widow is to beb put on the list only if...." According to *Thayer's Greek-English Lexicon of the New Testament,* this exclusive list was comprised "of those widows who held a prominent place in the church and exercised a certain superintendence over the rest of the women, and had charge of the widows and orphans supported at the public expense" (Thayer, s.v. *katalego,* Strong's #2639).

11 Thayer, s.v. *timao,* Strong's #5091.

12 Platz, pp. 116-118.

13 Ibid, pp. 135-137.

14 Strong's #5293; *Hupotasso.*

15 *Interlinear Study Bible,* http://www.studylight.org/isb/bible.cgi?query= pr+3%3A6&section=)&it=nas&oq=pr%25203%3A6&ot=bhs&nt=na &new=1&nb=pr&ng=3&ncc=3>accessed September 2004, s.v. *yada,* Strongs #3045.

16 Platz, pp. 163-165.

Bibliography

Ask Dr. Sears, http://www.askdrsears.com.

Easton, Matthew George. *Easton's Bible Dictionary,* http://www.studylight.org/dic/ebd/, 1897.

Platz, Ann. *The Best is Yet to Come:* Designing Your Future With Style. Birmingham, Alabama: New Hope Publishers, 2005.

Strong, James. *Strong's Exhaustive Concordance of the Bible,* "Greek Dictionary of the New Testament" (Nashville: TN, Thomas Nelson Publishers, 1990).

Thayer, Joseph H. *Thayer's Greek-English Lexicon of the New Testament.* Peabody, Massachusetts: Hendrickson Publishers, October 2003.

About the Contributors

Emily Steele has a desire to help authors communicate their ideas through the written word. She began working in the editorial department at Harrison House in 1997. After the arrival of her firstborn, she became a work-at-home mom, writing, editing, and proofreading for a number of publishers while also caring for her beautiful daughter. Today, along with her husband, Matt, and two energetic children, Kaela and Jaron, she now resides in the Los Angeles area.

Ann Platz has been well-known in the South as an interior designer for over twenty-five years and is a popular and delightful lecturer. Speaking on topics from design and etiquette to the deeper things of the Spirit, Ann warms the heart with her effortless southern elegance and storytelling wit. She is the author of six other books, including *Social Graces* and *The Pleasure of Your Company*. Ann currently resides in Atlanta, Georgia, with her husband, John. She is the mother of two daughters and the grandmother of six grandchildren.

Sue Anne Allen is a mother of four who tackles parenthood with her husband, Steve, in Atlanta, Georgia. With a B.A. in Psychology and an M.A. in Human Development, Sue is a Marriage and Family Therapist and a Play Therapy Supervisor. After journaling daily for 17 years, Sue recently gave birth to her first book, entitled *Scribbling A Masterpiece: Doodle To Your Destiny*. You may contact Sue online at www.spreadinggodsspirit.com.

Nancy B. Gibbs is the author of four books, editor, motivational speaker, weekly religion columnist for two newspapers, and a writer. She has been published in hundreds of books, devotional guides, and magazines. Nancy is a pastor's wife, mother, and grandmother. She may be reached at Daiseydood@aol.com or through her Web site at Nancybgibbs.com.

Tracie Hunsberger is a wife and mother of four, is a Rhema Bible School Graduate, and is currently employed by Harrison House Publishers. She also works with Daughters of Destiny at the Tulsa Dream Center, a program set up for disadvantaged girls, ages 9-14, guiding them into the purpose that God has for their lives. She also conducts fundraisers to raise support for the disadvantaged families in the community. Tracie enjoys speaking and ministering to preteen and teenage girls. You may contact Tracie at ethunsberger@aol.com.

Karen Kilby resides in Kingwood, Texas, with her husband, David. As a Certified Personality Trainer with CLASServices, Inc., Karen enjoys helping people understand themselves and others through her seminar presentations. Karen is also a speaker for Christian Women's Clubs with Stonecroft Ministries and has had several of her stories published. Karen can be reached at krkilby@kingwoodcable.net.

Julie Lechlider currently works as the Managing Editor of Harrison House Publishers and serves as a volunteer for New Life Children's Home, a network of Christian orphanages in the Philippines and Nepal. Julie and her husband, Scott, make their home in Oklahoma with their two beautiful daughters, Haley and Abbey.

Marilyn Nutter has been a faculty member at Christian colleges in the field of communication disorders for the past 23 years. Currently, she serves as a MOPS mentor and a Bible study teacher for women's ministries in her local church. She is also a partner in *Shepherd's Cup,* a tea-based ministry, presents seminars, and enjoys tea parties. She has been married for 35 years, has three grown daughters and a granddaughter, and lives with her husband, Randy, in western Pennsylvania.

Kathy Pride is a mom, writer, speaker, and parent educator. Her first book, *Hope For Parents: When Drugs Seduce Your Teens,* is being published by AMG in 2005. Kathy has a passion for encouraging individuals to take the tatters and loose ends of their lives and weave them into lives of new possibility. She is the Founder and Director of Tapestry Ministry, and can be reached at Kathy@Tapestryministry.com.

Sheila Small and her husband, Bernard, divide their time between their homes in New York and New Jersey. Sheila's full-time pleasure is serving the Lord, being a wife, mother, and grandmother. She also enjoys spending time with her expanded family of brothers and sisters in Christ and writing.

Prayer of Salvation

God loves you—no matter who you are, no matter what your past. God loves you so much that He gave His one and only begotten Son for you. The Bible tells us that "...whoever believes in him shall not perish but have eternal life" (John 3:16). Jesus laid down His life and rose again so that we could spend eternity with Him in heaven and experience His absolute best on earth. If you would like to receive Jesus into your life, say the following prayer out loud and mean it from your heart.

Heavenly Father, I come to You admitting that I am a sinner. Right now, I choose to turn away from sin, and I ask You to cleanse me of all unrighteousness. I believe that Your Son, Jesus, died on the cross to take away my sins. I also believe that He rose again from the dead so that I might be forgiven of my sins and made righteous through faith in Him. I call upon the name of Jesus Christ to be the Savior and Lord of my life. Jesus, I choose to follow You and ask that You fill me with the power of the Holy Spirit. I declare that right now I am a child of God. I am free from sin and full of the righteousness of God. I am saved in Jesus' name. Amen.

If you prayed this prayer to receive Jesus Christ as your Savior for the first time, please contact us on the Web at **www.harrisonhouse.com** to receive a free book.

Or you may write to us at

Harrison House
P.O. Box 35035
Tulsa, Oklahoma 74153

Live the Life You Were Born to Live

Destiny is built on thousands of moments—opportunities to seek God's will, to seek His direction in the experience of every day. Let the Life on Purpose Series encourage you to make the most of every moment.

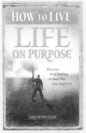

How to Live Your Life on Purpose™
ISBN 1-57794-321-X

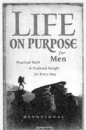

Life on Purpose™ for Women
ISBN 1-57794-649-9

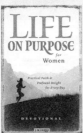

Life on Purpose™ for Men
ISBN 1-57794-648-0

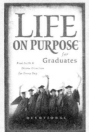

Life on Purpose™ for Graduates
ISBN 1-57794-727-4

www.harrisonhouse.com

Fast. Easy. Convenient!

- ◆ New Book Information
- ◆ Look Inside the Book
- ◆ Press Releases
- ◆ Bestsellers

- ◆ Free E-News
- ◆ Author Biographies
- ◆ Upcoming Books
- ◆ Share Your Testimony

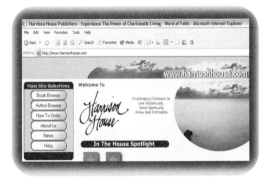

For the latest in book news and author information, please visit us on the Web at www.harrisonhouse.com. Get up-to-date pictures and details on all our powerful and life-changing products. Sign up for our e-mail newsletter, *Friends of the House,* and receive free monthly information on our authors and products including testimonials, author announcements, and more!

Harrison House—
Books That Bring Hope, Books That Bring Change

The Harrison House Vision

Proclaiming the truth and the power

Of the Gospel of Jesus Christ

With excellence;

Challenging Christians to

Live victoriously,

Grow spiritually,

Know God intimately.